A Glimpse At Early Christian Church Life

A Modern English Rendition
Of Writings of
Tertullian
from the translations of S. Thelwall

ISBN: 092-4722-037

Library of Congress Catalog No. 90-062563

Cover illustration: ©Robyn Miller, 1990
Cover design: Robyn Miller

Printed in the United States of America

To my son Isaiah.
May you always say, "Here am I. Send me!"

Contents

On The Veiling Of Virgins

About This Translation

Next to the Bible, the writings of the early Christians (A.D. 90-325) are the most valuable documents of Christianity. Like the Bible, they are part of the heritage of all Christians. Although these writings are not inspired, Scroll Publishing Co. believes that any translation of them should be undertaken as carefully as that of the Scriptures.

To that end, our contemporary renditions have been taken from the scholarly, careful translations that comprise *The Ante-Nicene Christian Library*. These translations were first published in 1867, in Edinburgh, Scotland, under the editorial supervision of Alexander Roberts, D.D., and James Donaldson, LL.D. As expressed by those editors, their objective was "to place the English reader as nearly as possible on a footing of equality with those who are able to read the original. With this view they [the translators] have for the most part leaned towards literal exactness; and wherever any considerable departure from this has been made, a verbatim rendering has been given at the foot of the page" (from the Preface to *The Ante-Nicene Christian Library*).

It was precisely this "literal exactness" that persuaded us to use, as the basis for this work, the translations made by the Rev. S. Thelwall for *The Ante-Nicene Christian Library*. We see little value in publishing a version of the early Christian writings that has been colored by the interpretations and theological biases of the translator. On the other hand, although we applaud the "literal exactness" of the *Ante-Nicene* translations, we realize that their stilted, archaic language discourages the modern layperson from reading them.

Therefore, the goal of Scroll Publishing is to render the early Christian works into contemporary, readable English while preserving the meaning of the original writers. To this end, we have followed a two-tiered system in our renditions:

We have been very strict in rendering passages containing material of theological, ecclesiastical, or moral significance to the modern reader. In such passages, we have aimed at "literal exactness," concentrating on faithfully communicating the writer's actual words or phraseology. However, we have paraphrased those passages that do *not* contain anything of theological, ecclesiastical, or moral significance to the modern reader. In such passages, we have concentrated on capturing as exactly as possible the meaning of the original writer, using simpler, more contemporary language.

We have sometimes deleted sentences, clauses or paragraphs that are repetitious or whose meaning is obscure. For the sake of abridgement, several entire chapters from *The Shows* have been deleted. However, any such deletions are marked with an alphabetical superscript, and all such deleted material has been reprinted in the appendix at the back of the book.

This volume contains five tracts or sermons of Tertullian: *The Shows, On Prayer, On The Apparel Of Women (Book Two), On Baptism,* and *On The Veiling Of Virgins*. To enhance the readability of these works, the modern editor has furnished all chapter titles, subheadings, and footnotes. (However, the chapter divisions used in *The Ante-Nicene Christian Library* have been marked throughout the text with Arabic numbers.) The modern editor has also supplied all Scripture citations. There were no Scripture citations in the original texts. In fact, the Scriptures had not yet been divided into chapters and verses when Tertullian wrote these works.

This revised edition of S. Thelwall's translations was prepared by David W. Bercot. He obtained his Bachelor of Arts degree summa cum laude from Stephen F. Austin University and his Doctor of Jurisprudence degree cum laude from Baylor University School of Law. The early Christian writings have been his special field of study for a number of years. He is the author of the book, *Will The Real Heretics Please Stand Up*, which concerns the early Christians. He has also written articles for various journals about the early church and frequently lectures on the subject of early Christianity. Pam Warren and Jim Shaw, staff writers with Youth With A Mission, assisted Mr. Bercot on parts of this rendition.

The Armchair Time Traveler

One of the most popular themes in science fiction today is time travel. Probably all of us have at one time or another yearned to be able to travel back in time to visit a century long removed from our own. But, as of yet, no one has invented a time machine. So the closest thing we have to time travel is reading the works of persons who lived in a different era from our own.

This book equips you to take a glimpse at church life around A.D. 200. It is not some fanciful, largely fictitious account of how the early Christians lived and worshipped in the early centuries. Instead, it is a collection of five of Tertullian's sermons and tracts that honestly reveal many of the customs, beliefs, worship practices, controversies, and lifestyle of the early Christians. Tertullian composed these works between A.D. 195 and 210.

As you will see from reading these writings, when Christianity was young, church life extended far beyond the walls of the meeting house. It touched personal prayer life, entertainment, work, dress, and every other aspect of a Christian's life. Through his writings, Tertullian gives us insight into the complete sphere of Christian life in the early centuries of Christianity.

Tertullian: Contender For God

Tertullian was born around A.D. 150 in the city of Carthage in North Africa. Both of his parents were pagan, and his father was a centurion. Tertullian received a thorough education in the knowledge of the Romans and the Greeks, and he apparently practiced law before his conversion. His writings indicate that he did not become a Christian until he was in his thirties or forties.[1]

However, once Tertullian gave his life to Christ, he held nothing back. Like Paul, he viewed all of his worldly education and social rank as "dung" in relation to the things of Christ. At the same time, he used his vast learning in the cause of Christ. At the risk of his life, he wrote several works to the Romans, defending Christianity and attempting to persuade the authorities to halt their senseless persecution.

Tertullian apparently served as an elder or presbyter in Carthage, completely devoting his life to the ministry of Christ. Not only did he write apologetic works to the Romans, but he also composed a considerable number of writings in which he defended orthodox Christianity against various heretics. In other writings, he attacked the growing spiritual laxity he saw developing in the church.

The New Testament was written in Greek, and up until the time of Tertullian nearly all other Christian works had likewise been written in Greek. Although Tertullian was fluent in Greek and wrote several works in Greek, he penned most of his works in Latin—in order to benefit the growing number of western Christians who knew only Latin. As a result, Tertullian often had to develop Latin terminology to express the truths that had previously been presented primarily in the Greek language. The most famous of his newly coined terms was the word "Trinity," which has become a standard term in the Christian vocabulary.

Warning: Tertullian's Writings Will Probably Offend You

Because of his fiery temperament and forceful convictions, nearly all of Tertullian's writings have polemic overtones. Church historian Phillip Schaff said of him: "He resembled a foaming mountain torrent rather than a calm, transparent river in the valley. His vehement temper was never fully subdued, although he struggled sincerely against it. He was a man of strong convictions, and never hesitated to express them without fear or favor. ...His polemics everywhere leave marks of blood. It is a wonder that he was not killed by the heathens."[2]

Tertullian's style was to attack, rather than to gently persuade. Every time I read his works I find myself wanting to spar with him verbally. You will probably have the same reaction. However, it will be to your benefit if you will resist the urge to do that. Remember, you are simply an armchair time traveler listening in on sermons and arguments of the second and third centuries. As such, your first task is to know and understand the practices and beliefs—and controversies—of the early Christians.

After all, what Tertullian believed is not, in itself, that important. What is important is what *the apostles* believed—and what they taught to others. In other words, the issue is not what Tertullian believed, but what *we* should believe. So instead of wasting your time arguing with Tertullian, I encourage you to temporarily put aside your own views and preconceptions. Instead, study the Scripture passages upon which Tertullian based his arguments. Listen with an honest and open heart to what the apostles said. Most of Tertullian's views are solidly based on Scripture, but not all of them. We Christians are under no obligation to follow Tertullian's personal views, but we are obligated to be obedient to Christ and his apostles.

Tertullian's works on entertainment, adornment, and women's prayer coverings will not be popular with most of today's American Christians. We are used to having the Scripture passages on those subjects explained away or simply ignored. As a result, Tertullian comes across to us as a puritanical fanatic and a male chauvinist. However, perhaps Tertullian's primary crime is that he took the teachings of the apostles very literally and very seriously.

And he wasn't alone in doing that. Virtually all of the early Christian writers did. In fact, Tertullian's eastern contemporary, Clement of Alexandria, taught practically the same things on entertainment and adornment as did Tertullian. The difference is that Clement generally presented things more gently and lovingly than did Tertullian. Tertullian's temperament and personality fall considerably short of that of Christ. He is one of the harshest of all the early Christian writers. Yet, his writings are invaluable because they give us a record of the viewpoints, issues and controversies that concerned the church in his day.

One final point should be mentioned. Tertullian often said things sarcastically or rhetorically. As a result, he sometimes purposefully said just the opposite of what he was arguing. His *hearers*, of course, realized what things he was saying sarcastically. However, his *readers* have a much more difficult time discerning this. So if you suddenly come upon a statement that seems to say the opposite of what Tertullian has been arguing, he probably intended for his statement to be understood in a sarcastic sense.

I do not endorse or accept everything that Tertullian said, nor the spirit in which he said them. At the same time, he has opened my eyes to a lot of areas in my life that needed correction. A surgeon's knife is painful, but it can save lives. If spiritual surgery is needed in your life, I hope that God will use these writings as an instrument of His loving correction.

David W. Bercot
Editor

---

[1]Philip Schaff, *History of the Christian Church*, vol. 2 (Grand Rapids: Wm. B. Eerdmans, 1910), p. 820.

[2]*Ibid.*, pp. 822-824

The Shows

1

Why Christians Should Avoid The Shows

1. You servants of God, who are about to draw near to God,[1] are doing so to make a solemn dedication of yourselves to him. Therefore, you need to seek diligently to understand the conditions of faith, the reasons of the Truth, and the laws of Christian discipline. These three things forbid the pleasures of the public shows, along with other sins of the world.

And those of you who have already testified and confessed that you have done so,[2] still need to review this subject. The reason is so that you won't sin because of ignorance—whether unintentional or willful. The power of earthly pleasures is great. As a result, our flesh contrives ways for us to remain willfully ignorant. That way, we can continue to indulge in such pleasures. In effect, our flesh bribes Knowledge to be dishonest.

---

[1] i.e. those who are preparing for baptism.

[2] i.e., renounced the world; here Tertullian is addressing those who are already baptized.

Arguments Made By Pagans

Perhaps some of you are lured by the reasonings of the pagans, who pressure us with various arguments. Two of their arguments are as follows: First, that religion is in the *mind* and the *conscience*. Therefore it does not oppose the exquisite pleasures the eyes and ears receive from *external* things. And secondly, that surely God is not offended by any human enjoyment or pleasures so long as all due honor and reverence are given to him. For, they argue, these things are not sinful to partake of in their own times and places. However, I'm precisely ready to prove that these things are not consistent with true religion and genuine obedience to the true God.

It is well known that Christians are a sort of people who are always ready to die. Therefore, some people imagine that the sole purpose of our training in the type of abstinence[3] we practice is so it will be easier for us to give up this life. In other words, they think our abstinence already severs our ties to the present life. They regard our abstinence as an art of quenching all desire for life. For as far as they are concerned, we have emptied life of all those things that make it desirable.[4]

So they view our abstinence as merely a matter of human planning and foresight. However, in truth it is something clearly laid down by divine command. To be sure, it would be a grievous thing for Christians to die for God while enjoying the sumptuous pleasures [of this life]. Nevertheless, it is still not as the pagans say.[a]

2. Another argument that everyone throws at us is as follows: We teach that all things were created by God, and that they were given to man for his use. Therefore, all things must be good, for they come from such a good Source. And, all of these "good things" make up the public shows: horses,

---

[3]i.e., abstinence from worldly pleasures.

[4]This echoes the well-known sentiments of the Romans, who viewed Christians as "enemies of the human race."

lions, bodily strength, and musical voices. So we cannot think that what exists by God's own creative will is either foreign to him or opposed to him. And if it is not opposed to him, it cannot be viewed as something harmful to his worshipers. For it is certainly not foreign to them.

They continue with their argument, saying that the very buildings made for public amusement are constructed of rocks, stones, marble, and pillars. And these are things of God. For God has enriched the earth with these things. In fact, the very spectacles take place under God's own heaven.

Human wisdom seems ever wise in her own eyes. This is particularly true if she has the fear of losing any of her delights. That is, any of the sweet enjoyments of worldly existence. In fact, there are quite a few persons who hold back from becoming Christians—not because they are afraid of losing their *lives*—but because they are afraid of losing their *pleasures*. For even a weakling has no strong fear of death as a debt that must be paid. However, the [worldly]-wise man prizes pleasure. He regards it as a precious gift. He sees it as one of the true blessings of life, available to philosopher and fool alike.

The Christian Response

Of course, nobody denies that God is the Maker of the universe. Everybody knows this, for Nature itself teaches us this. And so the universe is good, and God gave it to man as a free gift. However, unbelievers know God only by natural revelation. They have no intimate relationship with the Highest. They do not know him as friends. They do not know him as do those who have been brought close to him. Knowing him only from afar, unbelievers cannot help but be ignorant of what God commands to be done. Nor can they know what he forbids regarding the administration of his world.

Likewise, they are necessarily ignorant of the hostile power that works against God. This power perverts the things God's hand has formed and uses them for wrong. If you do not know God, you cannot perceive either his will or his adversary. It is not enough to merely know who made all things. We must also know who perverted all things. When we discover what creation was *not* made for, we can find out what it *was* made for. There is a vast difference between the present corrupted state and the original state of purity. That's because there is a vast difference between the Creator and the corrupter. All kinds of evil have come from what was originally the work of God. And these are evils that even the pagans prohibit. In fact, they guard themselves from these things.

Take murder for example. It can be committed by iron,[5] by poison, or by magical enchantments. Now, iron, herbs, and demons were all created by God. But did the Creator provide those things for man's destruction? No! Rather, he prohibited every type of man-killing with that one concise commandment, "You shall not kill." (Ex. 20:13)

Moreover, wasn't it God, the Maker of the world, who placed in the world all of its gold, brass, silver, ivory, wood, and all the other materials that are used to make idols? Yet, did he do this so that man could establish worship contrary to Himself? On the contrary, idolatry is one of the greatest of sins in His eyes. Everything offensive to God was originally something He made. Yet, in offending God, it ceases to be His. And when it ceases to be His, it becomes something injurious in His eyes.

Look at man himself! He is guilty of every sin; yet he is not only a work of God—he is His image. Nevertheless, both in body and soul man has severed himself from his Maker. God didn't give us eyes to lust with. He didn't give us the tongue for speaking evil. He didn't create ears so that we could hear evil speech. He didn't make the throat and stomach for the purpose of gluttony. The genitals weren't made for unchaste conduct. Neither were hands made to enact violence, nor feet to follow a sinful life. Finally, the soul wasn't placed in the body so that it could think of evil snares, fraud, and injustice.

Of course not! For God is the One who requires innocence. He hates everything that even *resembles* malice. He utterly hates the planning of evil. Obviously, none of the things that have

---

[5]i.e., the sword or spear.

come from his hand were made to be used for purposes that he condemns.[b] Therefore, we who have obtained knowledge of the Lord have also obtained some knowledge of his foe.[c] In the beginning, the prowess of the corrupting and God-opposing angel overturned the virtue of man, who was the handiwork and image of God, and the possessor of the world. So we should neither marvel nor doubt the fact that this angel has entirely changed man's nature. Like the original nature of that angel, man's nature was created for perfect sinlessness. But the angel has changed man's nature into the present nature of the angel—a state of wicked enmity against his Maker. He did this so that[d] he might make man guilty in God's eyes, and set up his own supremacy.

The Arguments Of Some Christians

3. Having answered the reasonings of the pagans, let us now turn to the unworthy reasonings of our own people. For the faith of some Christians is either too simple or overly scrupulous. They demand direct authority from Scripture for giving up the shows. They say that the matter is unclear, since such abstinence is not clearly imposed on God's servants in specific language.

Of course, we are never going to find it expressed with the same specificity as "You shall not kill, you shall not worship an idol, or you shall not commit adultery or fraud." (Ex. 20:14) There isn't a commandment, "You shall not enter the circus or the theater." Or "You shall not watch a [gladiatorial] combat or a stage play." Nevertheless, we do find that the first words of David [in the Psalms] apply to this very sort of thing: "Blessed," he says, "is the man who has not gone into the assembly of the wicked, nor stood in the way of sinners, nor sat in the chair of mockers." (Ps. 1:1)

Avoiding 'The Assembly Of The Wicked'

Apparently, David was primarily prophesying about the righteous man who would take no part in the meetings and deliberations of the Jews who were plotting the death of our Lord. Nevertheless, divine Scripture has ever far-reaching applications. After the immediate sense of a Scripture is exhausted, the Scripture still reaches out in all directions to fortify the practice of the religious life. So, in the present instance, you have a saying that is not far from a plain prohibition of the shows.

If David referred to a handful of Jews as "an assembly of the wicked," how much more so would he refer to a vast gathering of pagans [at the shows]. Are the pagans less wicked than the Jews were then? Are they, in any less degree, sinners or enemies of Christ? Notice too how other portions of this Scripture fit an application to the shows. For at the shows also, people "stand in the way." For they refer to the spaces between the seats, which go around the amphitheater, as "ways." They also refer to the passages, which separate the people running down, as "ways." And the place in the curve where the matrons sit is called a "chair."

Therefore, on the contrary, the Scripture teaches that *any* person who has entered *any* assembly of wicked men is not blessed. Likewise, anyone who has stood in any way of sinners, and who has sat in any chair of mockers, is not blessed. We can understand something [in Scripture] to have been spoken in general terms, even though the primary application is to a specific subject. Some things that were spoken with a special situation in mind also contain general truths. For example, when God admonished the Israelites to fulfill their duty, or when he sharply rebuked them, he was surely referring to *all* men. When he threatened destruction to Egypt and Ethiopia, he was surely condemning in advance every sinning nation whatever. If we reason from the special to the general, every nation that sins is an Egypt and Ethiopia. Likewise, when we reason from the specific to the general with regards to the topic of shows, every show is an assembly of the wicked.

2

The Origin Of The Shows

4. However, someone may think that I am merely dealing in subtleties of argument. So let me point to the very high authority of our "seal" itself.[1] When we enter the water, we make confession of the Christian faith in the words of its rule. We publicly confess that we have renounced the devil, his pomp, and his angels.[2] Now, isn't the devil, along with his pomp and his angels, primarily connected with idolatry? And, in short, every unclean and wicked spirit comes from idolatry.

So, if I can demonstrate that everything connected with the shows is based on idolatry, then it will be manifestly evident that our confession in the bath of baptism applies to the shows. For, through their idolatry, the shows have been handed over to the devil, his pomp, and his angels.

Accordingly, I am going to discuss the various origins of the shows. I will show, so to speak, from what nursing places they have progressed to adulthood. Then I will discuss the titles of some of the shows—that is, by what names they are

---

[1]ie., baptism.

[2]In the early church, a candidate for baptism would make public confession of Christ and would also publicly testify, "I renounce the devil, his pomp, and his angels." This is very similar to the procedure still used by the Orthodox Church when baptizing adults.

called. Next, I will move to the ceremonies, demonstrating with what superstitions they are observed. Then I will discuss their locations and to what patrons they are dedicated. Finally, I will point out the arts that minister to the shows and to what authors they can be traced.

Now, if any of the shows shall be found to have had no connection with any idol god, then I will acknowledge that they are free from the taint of idolatry. And thus they do not come under the sphere of our baptismal renunciation.

The Origin Of The Games

5. [In chapters five through eleven of his tract, Tertullian discussed the origins of the various types of shows: the athletic games, the chariot races, the theaters, gymnastic exhibitions, and the gladiatorial combats. He showed that all of these shows were steeped in pagan idolatry from the very beginning. These chapters have been reproduced in their entirety in the appendix.[e] However, we have set forth below some key excerpts from these chapters:]

The origins of the shows are somewhat obscure, and many among us know little about them. For that reason, our investigation must go back to remote antiquity. Our authorities can be none other than the actual books of pagan literature. Various authors have published works on this subject, which works are still in existence.

According to them, the origin of the games is as follows: Timaeus tells us that immigrants from Asia...had settled down in Etruria.[3] In their new home, these people set up public shows. These were set up in addition to other superstitious observances under the name of religion. On their own request, the Romans obtained from these people skilled performers. ...The Romans also obtained the name *Ludi* from them, for it is said that the name was derived from *Lydi*.[4]

---

[3]Etruria, the home of the Etruscans, was an ancient country in the central part of western Italy.

[4]The Romans called their games or sporting events *ludi*. The Asian immigrants that Tertullian is discussing were apparently from Lydia, a country in Asia Minor.

However, Varro[5] said the name *Ludi* comes from *ludus*, which means "play" or "game." ...Even if that is the case, Varro still viewed the sporting games of young men to belong to festal days, temples, and objects of religious worship. Of course, the exact origin of the *name* is not that important when it is clear that the games spring from idolatry.[6]

The other public games have their religious origin in the birthdays and ceremonies of kings, and in public victories on municipal holidays. There are also games held in memory of the dead. In these, funereal honors are rendered to private individuals. This is a custom that dates back to ancient times. For from the very first, there were two types of public games. There was the sacred, in honor of pagan gods. And there was the funereal, in honor of the dead.

But as far as idolatry, it makes no difference to us which name or title the games are played under. Either way, the games are connected with the wicked spirits we renounce. If it is lawful to offer reverence to the dead, it is just as lawful to offer it to the gods of the dead. In both cases, you have the same origin, the same idolatry. And for our part, we have the same solemn renunciation of all idolatry.[7]

The Origin Of The Chariot Races

Next, in the course of discussing the *places* where the shows are held, I will discuss the circus.[8] The circus is primarily consecrated to the Sun. In fact, a temple to the Sun stands in the middle of the circus. ...

And, speaking of places, this will be an appropriate time to address some of the questions I anticipate will be raised. You may say, "Am I in danger of pollution if I only go into the circus when the races are *not* being celebrated?" No, for there is no law prohibiting the mere *places* to us. In fact, the servant of God, without any peril to his religion, may enter

[5]Marcus Varro (116-27 B.C.) was the greatest scholar of the Roman Republic.

[6]The preceding two paragraphs are from chap. 5 of *The Shows*.

[7]The two foregoing paragraphs are from chap. 6 of *The Shows*.

[8]The circus was the oval-shaped race course where the chariot races were held.

not only the places of the shows, but even the temples! That is, if he has some honest reason for being there, unconnected with the normal transactions and official duties that take place there. For that matter, even the streets, the market places, the baths, the inns, and our very dwelling places are not totally free from idols. Satan and his angels have filled the whole world!

However, it is not by merely being *in* the world that we fall away from God. It is by touching and tainting ourselves with the world's sins. I separate myself from my Maker if I go to the Capitol[9] or the temple of Serapis to sacrifice or worship. And I do the same by going to the circus and the theater as a spectator. The places themselves do not contaminate. It is what is *done* in them that contaminates. And because of what is done in them, we maintain that the places themselves have become defiled.

The polluted things pollute us. It is for this reason that I have shown you to whom these various places have been dedicated. In that manner, you can realize that the things done in them belong to the idol gods to whom these places are considered sacred.[10]

Now let me address the type of performances that are unique to the circus shows. In former days, equestrianism was practiced in a simple way on horseback. And certainly, in its ordinary use, it had nothing sinful about it. But when it was dragged into the games, it passed from the service of God into the employment of demons.[11]

The Origin Of The Theater

So we have first discussed the origin of the games, and from there progressed to the circus shows. Now we will take a look at the theater, beginning with the places where theatrical plays are staged. At first, the theater was properly a temple of Venus. And it was for this reason that stage perfor-

[9]The temple of Jupiter on the Capitoline Hill in Rome.

[10]The preceding three paragraphs are from chap. 8 of *The Shows*.

[11]The preceding paragraph is from chap. 9 of *The Shows*.

mances were allowed to escape censure. That is how the theater got its foothold in the world. Yet, oftentimes, in the interests of morality, the censors tried to put down the rising theaters. They foresaw that there was great danger that the theaters would lead to a general moral abandonment. This should be quite a testimony to the pagans. For originally, their own people held to a view that is similar to ours. And their human judgment, based on foresight, is actually a confirmation of our views.[12]

The Origin Of The Gladiator Contests

12. Now we come to the most noted spectacle, the one the people like the most.[13] They sometimes call this spectacle *munus*, which means "duty." Other times, they call it *officium*, which means "service." The ancients thought they were rendering service to the dead through this ceremony.

At a later period, with a more "refined" cruelty, they somewhat modified the character of this spectacle. For, at first, the ancients were in the habit of buying captives or slaves of wicked character and then sacrificing them in their cremation rites. They did this because they believed that the souls of the departed were appeased by human blood. However, later they decided to turn their iniquity into something pleasurable.

So, to the best of their ability, they trained their sacrificial victims in the use of weapons. Of course, they trained them only so that these victims could learn how to die properly. On their funeral day, these victims were killed at the places of their cremations. So the ancients murdered others in an effort to alleviate their own deaths! And that is the origin of the gladiator games. But by degrees, the "refinement" of the ancients came up to their cruelty. For these vicious human beasts were not satisfied until they could watch men being torn to pieces by wild animals.

---

[12]The preceding paragraph is from chap. 10 of *The Shows*.

[13]Tertullian is now speaking of the gladiatorial contests.

Offerings to appease the dead were regarded at that time as belonging to the class of cremation sacrifices. And such sacrifices are idolatry. For idolatry, in fact, is a sort of reverence for the departed. The one as well as the other is a service to dead men. Moreover, demons dwell in the images of the dead.[f]

What need, then, is there for me to dwell on this place of horrors. It's too terrible even for the tongue of a liar. For the amphitheater is dedicated to gods more numerous and more horrible than is even the Capitol, which itself is the temple of all demons.[14] There are as many unclean spirits in the amphitheater as it holds men. To conclude with a single remark about the skills that have a place in it, we know that its two sorts of amusement have for their patron deities, Mars and Diana.[15]

---

[14]The amphitheater, the place where gladiatorial contests were held, was dedicated to Pluto and other gods of the underworld.

[15]Mars was the god of war, and Diana was the goddess of woods, women, and childbirth. Diana was believed to cause the death of women, sometimes in a cruel manner (such as was practiced in the amphitheater).

3

God's Table And The Table Of Demons

13. I think I have now faithfully carried out my plan of demonstrating how the sin of idolatry clings to the shows in various ways: their origins, titles, equipment, places of celebration, and their arts. Beyond all doubt, they are unsuitable for us who have doubly renounced all idols. "Not that an idol is anything," as the apostle says, but that the reverence rendered to them is actually rendered to demons. (1 Cor. 8:4) For the demons are the real occupants of these consecrated images, whether of dead men or (as they think) of gods.

Actually, their dead and their deities are one and the same. For this reason, we abstain from both idolatries. For both have a common source. Nor do we dislike the temples less than the monuments of the dead. We have nothing to do with either altar. We worship neither image. We do not offer sacrifices to the gods. And we make no funeral sacrifices to the departed.[8] For we cannot partake of God's feast and the feast of devils. (1 Cor. 10:21)

We keep our throats and stomachs free from such defilements.[1] How much more so should we withhold our more noble parts—our eyes and ears—from the idolatrous and

---

[1]The early Christians followed the apostolic commandment to "abstain from things offered to idols." (Acts 15:29)

funereal enjoyments. To be sure, these enjoyments do not pass through the body. Yet, they are digested into the very spirit and soul. And God has a right to claim from us purity of spirit and soul—even more so than that of our bodily organs.

14. I think I have sufficiently established the charge of idolatry against the shows. And that alone should be reason enough for our giving up the shows. However, in order to establish our case beyond doubt, let's look at the subject in another way. This will particularly be for those who are comfortable with their position that the abstinence we urge is not commanded [in Scripture] in specific words.

We Should Not Lust For Things Of The World

The condemnation of the lusts of the world should be sufficient to rule out all of these amusements. (1 John 2:15,16) For there is such a thing as a lust for pleasure, just as much so as a lust for money, social position, banqueting, immorality, or glory. And the shows are just a type of pleasure. I think then that the general designation of "lusts" includes pleasures.[h]

15. I now want to contrast the other characteristics of the shows with the things of God. God has instructed us to deal calmly, gently, quietly, and peacefully with the Holy Spirit. (Phil. 4:8) For only these things are befitting the goodness of his nature—with his tenderness and feeling. And He instructs us not to disturb Him with rage, evil dispositions, anger, or causes of grief. (Eph. 4:31)

Well, what does all of this have to do with the shows? The point is that the shows always lead to agitation of the spirit. For where there are pleasures, there are intense feelings. They are what give pleasure its zest. And where there are intense feelings, there is rivalry, with a zest of its own. And where there is rivalry, there is rage, bitterness, wrath, and grief—together with all of the bad things that flow from them. The whole thing is entirely out of harmony with the religion of Christ. (Col. 3:8)

But let's suppose that one were to enjoy the shows in a *moderate* way. That is, in a way that befits his station in life, his age, or his nature. Still, such a person is not totally undisturbed in mind. There will still be some unuttered movings of the inner man. No one partakes of pleasures such as these without their strong excitements. And no one who comes under these excitements is free from the moral lapse that comes with them. Finally, these lapses create passionate desires.

On the other hand, if there were no desire, there would be no pleasure. And if someone goes where nothing is to be obtained, he can rightly be charged with being frivolous. And even that should be foreign to us, in my opinion. (Phil. 4:8) Moreover, a man condemns himself by the very act of joining in with those whom he confesses he is not in agreement with. He makes this confession by the fact he is disinclined to be like them. It is not enough simply to not share in such [wrongful] things ourselves. We must break all connection with those who do them. The Scripture says [in rebuke], "If you saw a thief, you joined in with him." (Ps. 50:18)

I wish that we did not even inhabit the same world as these wicked men! And although that wish cannot be realized, yet even now we are separate from them in what is *of* the world. (John 17:14) For the world is God's. But the *worldly* is the devil's.

4

How The Shows Pollute Us

16. All excitement that invokes violent emotion is forbidden to us. (Eph. 4:31) Therefore, we are barred from every kind of spectacle—especially the circus.[1] For violent emotions preside over the circus, as though they were at home there.

See the masses thronging to the circus, their violent emotions already aroused! They are already riotous, already blind with hysteria, already agitated about their bets! The master of the races is too slow for them. Their eyes are already rolling, as though they were among the lots in the master's urn. Everyone hangs on the edge of his seat, waiting for the signal. There is the united shout of a common madness.

Notice how their foolish speeches show how out of control they are. "He has thrown it!" they exclaim.[2] So each one announces to his neighbor what they have all seen alike. But actually they are all blind. They don't see what is *really* thrown. They think it is a signal cloth. But it is actually the image of the devil cast out from on high.[3] And accordingly,

---

[1]i.e., the chariot races.

[2]i.e., the master of the races has thrown the cloth, the signal for the charioteers to start the race.

[3]Tertullian apparently does not mean that the signal cloth is literally made in the image of Satan. Rather, he speaks figuratively.

the result is that they fly into rages, violent emotions, quarrels, and other things that those who are dedicated to peace should never indulge in.

Then there is cursing and booing—with no real cause for hatred. There are shouts of applause, with nothing to merit them.[i] Is a causeless love perhaps more legitimate than a causeless hatred? Yet, God clearly forbids us to hate another person, even when there is a reason for our hatred. Instead, he commands us to love our enemies. God forbids us to curse, even though there may be some grounds for doing so. Instead, we are to bless those who curse us. But what is more merciless than the circus, where people do not spare even their rulers and fellow citizens [from their curses]? If that sort of madness were befitting the saints of God in any other place, then I suppose it is all right to indulge in it at the circus. But if such madness is wrong in other places, then it is wrong at the circus as well.

The Theater

17. In like manner, aren't we also commanded to put away from us all immodesty? On that ground alone, we are barred from the theater. For the theater is the home of immodesty. Nothing is reputable in the theater except those things that are disreputable elsewhere. The highest favor of the god of the theater is won through the vulgarity of the comic's gestures. Or perhaps the vileness exhibited by the buffoon in woman's clothing, destroying all natural modesty. Actors blush more readily at home than at the play.[j]

Even the prostitutes, who are victims of the public lust, are brought upon the stage. Their wretchedness is increased by the fact that they are in the presence of other women. For it is only from other women that they are accustomed to hide themselves. These prostitutes are paraded publicly [on the stage] before every age group and social rank. Here, in the hearing of those who should not hear such things, the actors publicly declare the haunts, earnings, and praises of these prostitutes.

I say nothing about other matters, which are best left hidden in their own darkness and gloomy caves, lest they stain the light of day. Let the Senate, and all ranks, blush out of shame. Why, even these miserable women, who by their own gestures destroy their modesty, know something of shame at least once a year. At other times they dread the light of day and the gaze of people.

But if we should detest all that is immodest, on what grounds is it right for us to *hear* what we must not *speak*? For all lewd speech— in fact, every idle word—is condemned by God. (Eph. 5:3,4) In the same way, is it right to *look* upon that which is disgraceful to *do*? How is it that the things that defile a man when going out of his mouth, are not regarded as defiling him when they go in through his eyes and ears? For the eyes and ears are the personal attendants of the spirit. How can the spirit be pure when its personal attendants are impure? In short, when [Scripture] forbids immodesty, it forbids the theater.

We dismiss the teachings of secular literature as being foolishness in God's eyes don't we? (1 Cor. 3:19) So isn't it equally clear what our response should be to these spectacles? For the tragedies and comedies are both products of secular literature. Tragedies and comedies are the bloody, wanton, ungodly, and lewd inventors of crimes and lusts. Yet, it is not good for us even to recollect things that are atrocious and vile. (Phil. 4:8) What you reject in *deed*, you should not welcome in *word*.

Athletic Games

18. If you should argue that the track stadium is mentioned in Scripture, I will readily admit it.[4] But then you should admit that the things done there are not for you to look upon. I'm speaking of the blows, the kicks, the slaps, and all the recklessness of hand. I speak of all those things that disfigure the human face. For, in disfiguring it, a person disfigures nothing less than God's own image.

---

[4] Perhaps a reference to 2 Maccabees 4:3-20.

Naturally, you will never give your approval to those foolish races and throwing contests. Or, even less so, to the more foolish jumping feats. Nor will you find pleasure in injurious or useless exhibitions of strength. And certainly you will never approve those who strive after an artificial body[5] with the aim of surpassing the Creator's work.[k] And the wrestler's art is a devil's thing. For the devil wrestled with, and crushed to death, the first human beings. Wrestling skills are like the traits of the serpent: special holds, ways to clasp through twistings, and slippery defenses to glide away.

Finally, you have no need of crowns.[6] So why do you strive to get pleasures from crowns?

The Gladiator Fights

19. We shall now see how the Scriptures condemn the amphitheater. If we can establish that it is right to indulge in what is cruel, ungodly, and fierce, let us go there. If we are what pagans say we are, let us joyfully feast there on human blood.[7]

No doubt, it is right to have the guilty punished.[8] Who, but the criminal himself, would deny this. Yet, the innocent can find no pleasure in the suffering of another. Instead, he mourns that a human brother has sinned so heinously as to need a punishment so dreadful. But who can guarantee that it is always the guilty who are condemned to the wild beasts, or to some other doom? Who can guarantee that the innocent never suffer from the revenge of the judge, or the weakness of the defense presented? Who can guarantee that an innocent person didn't simply confess because he was unable to withstand the torture of the rack?

How much better, then, is it for me to remain ignorant of the punishment inflicted on the wicked. Otherwise, I am

---

[5]i.e., those who engage in body building to develop an unnaturally muscular body.

[6]The winners of the various athletic events received a laurel crown or wreath.

[7]Pagans accused Christians of practicing cannibalism at their meetings.

[8]Normally, the gladiators and those thrown to wild beasts were criminals.

obligated to also know about the good persons who come to untimely ends. That is, if I may speak of goodness in the case at all. Besides, there are gladiators who have not been charged with any crime, but are simply offered for sale for the public games. They thereby become the victims of public pleasure. Even in the case of those who are judicially condemned to the amphitheater, what a monstrous thing it is! For in undergoing their punishment, they advance from some less serious infraction to the crime of being manslayers.[9]

What I just said was addressed to pagans. I will not insult Christians by adding another word about the repugnance they should have for this type of spectacle. (However, few are more able than I to fully describe this whole subject, unless it be one who is still in the habit of going to the shows.[10]) I would rather leave this subject incomplete than to recollect such things.

---

[9]i.e., a gladiator could be successful only by killing another man—a crime in God's eyes.

[10]Apparently, before his conversion, Tertullian avidly attended the gladiator contests and other shows.

5

Be Not Unequally Yoked With Unbelievers

20. How vain—or should I say, how desperate—is the reasoning of those persons who, because they don't wish to lose some pleasure, argue that we cannot point to any specific words or specific place [in Scripture] where this avoidance is mentioned. They say there is no place [in Scripture] where the servants of God are directly forbidden to have anything to do with such gatherings.

Recently, I heard a novel argument by a certain man who loved the theatrical plays. He said, "The sun—and in fact, God himself—look down from heaven on the shows, and they aren't polluted thereby." Yes, and the sun also shines forth its rays on the common sewer without being defiled! As for God, would it be better if all transgressions were hidden from his eye so that we might all escape judgment? But God [not only looks down on the shows,] he looks upon robberies too. He sees falsehoods, adulteries, frauds, idolatries, and—yes—the shows. And for that very reason, *we* will not look at the shows, lest the All-Seeing see us as well.

You, oh man[1] are putting the criminal and the judge on the same level. The criminal is a criminal because he *is seen*. The

---

[1]i.e., the man who made this argument.

Judge is the judge because he *sees*. Are you saying that it is all right for us to act recklessly outside the boundaries of the circus? Is it all right for us to practice lewdness outside the gates of the theater? Is it right for us to act arrogantly outside the stadium, or to be cruel outside the amphitheater? Don't you know that God has eyes outside the entrances, balconies, and curtains of those shows? Nothing is free from blame if God condemns it, no matter where it is. It is never right—in any place—to do that which you may not do at *all* times and in *all* places.

Truth is only complete when it is free from the whims of opinion and varying judgments. Only when truth is free from such things can it claim full authority, unchanging reverence, and faithful obedience. Something that is truly good or truly evil cannot be anything but that. For in all things the truth of God is unchangeable.

Pagan Situational Ethics

21. The pagans do not have a full revelation of the truth because they are not taught by God. So they believe that a thing is evil or good depending on how it suits their self-will and emotions. Therefore, something that is good in one place is considered evil in another. And that which is evil in one place is considered good in another.

So oddly enough, the same man who is barely willing to lift up his tunic in public—even to relieve himself—takes it off in the circus, as though determined to expose himself before everybody. Or, the father who carefully protects and guards his virgin daughter's ears from every polluting word, personally takes her to the theater. He thereby exposes her to all its vile words and attitudes. Similarly, the same man who would seize or rebuke a brawling fighter in the streets, shouts encouragement to fights of a much more serious nature in the arena.

And finally, he who looks with horror on the corpse of someone who has died a natural death, calmly gazes in the amphitheater on bodies that are mangled, torn, and smeared with their own blood. In fact, the man who comes to the show because he thinks murderers should suffer for their crimes, drives the unwilling gladiator to the murderous deed with rods and whips. The one who demands that every manslayer of deeper dye be thrown to the lions, insists on the staff for the savage swordsman and rewards him with the cap of liberty.[2] Yes, and he [the spectator] must have the poor victim dragged back again so he can get a good look at his face. With zest he closely inspects the [dead] man whom he wished torn to pieces at a safe distance from him.[1]

Pagan Inconsistencies

22. How strange! Yet, we should expect such inconsistencies as these from men who confuse and change the nature of good and evil depending on their whims and fickleness in judgment. On the one hand, the playwrights and managers of the spectacles highly praise the charioteers, actors, wrestlers, and those most beloved gladiators, to whom men prostitute their souls and women prostitute their bodies. Yet, they then trample on them and treat them with indifference. They condemn these entertainers for doing the very deeds that were done for the sake of the playwrights and managers. They condemn them to shame and the loss of their rights as citizens, excluding them from the Senate house, from the speaker's platform at the Forum, from senatorial and equestrian rank, from certain social distinctions, and from all other honors.

What perversity! They take pleasure in those very persons they later penalize. They award their approval on those whom they later treat coldly. So they praise the art, but condemn the artist. What an outrage! They blacken a man for doing the very things that make him praiseworthy in their eyes. The fact that the performers, even when in the highest favor, are not without a mark of disgrace upon them is a confession that the shows themselves are evil.

23. Despite the sweetness of pleasure, mere human reflection leads men to believe that performers should be con-

---

[2]Gladiators who were successful in repeated combats often were given their freedom.

demned to a hapless lot of infamy. It leads them to believe that performers should lose all the advantages that go along with the dignities of life. This being the case, how much more so does the divine righteousness inflict punishment on those who give themselves to these arts.

Other Objections To The Shows

Do you think God has any pleasure in the charioteer who incites so many souls, who rouses so many furious emotions, and who creates so many various moods? The charioteer is sometimes crowned like a priest. Other times, he wears the colors of a pimp—decked out by the devil so he may be whirled away in his chariot, as though he were going to accompany Elijah.

Will God be pleased with the man who applies the razor to himself and completely changes his features? With no respect for his face, such a man is not content with merely making it as similar as possible to that of Saturn, Isis, and Bacchus.[3] Rather, he then peacefully surrenders it over to insulting blows, as if in mockery of our Lord. For the devil, too, makes it part of his teaching that the cheek is to be meekly offered to the one who hits.

Is Acting Appropriate For Christians?

In the same way, the devil has made the actors in the tragedies taller by having them wear platform shoes. Yet, Jesus had said, "No one can add a cubit to his height." (Matt. 6:27) So Satan seeks to make Christ a liar. What about the wearing of masks?[4] I must ask if that is in accordance with the mind of God. For He forbids the making of every type of likeness—particularly the likeness of man, who is God's own image. The Author of truth hates all that is false. Everything that is counterfeit, he regards as adultery. Since he condemns pretension in every form, he will never approve any putting

[3]The priests of Isis shaved their entire heads.

[4]Actors often wore masks on stage.

on of a pretended voice, sex, or age. Nor will he ever approve any pretended loves, wraths, groans, or tears.

Furthermore, in His Law, it is declared that a man who wears female clothing is accursed. (Deut. 22:5) So what must he think of a mime, who is even raised to play the role of a woman?[5]

And will the boxer go unpunished? I suppose he was created with those cestus[6] scars, heavily calloused fists, and cauliflower ears! And I also suppose that God gave him eyes for no other purpose than that they might be knocked out in fighting!

I say nothing of him who, to save himself, shoves someone else in the path of the lion. I suppose he does that so that when he puts that very same man to death in the arena, he won't appear to be only a small time murderer.

24. What else do I need to bring out to demonstrate that nothing characterizing the shows has God's approval? And if something does not have his approval, it is not appropriate for God's servants. Hopefully, I have succeeded in plainly demonstrating that the shows were instituted for the devil's sake. And hopefully I have demonstrated that the shows are composed entirely of the devil's things. For everything that is not of God, or that is not pleasing in His eyes, belongs to his wicked rival.

The Shows Contradict Our Baptismal Confession

Now, if I have demonstrated that all these things were instituted entirely for the devil's sake,[m] then it plainly means that in the shows you have the "pomp of the devil." And we renounce the "pomp of the devil" as part of the seal of our faith.[7] And we should have nothing to do with the things we renounce—whether in deed or in word. Whether by looking

[5]In ancient times, boys were sometimes specifically trained throughout their boyhood to play female roles on stage.

[6]A cestus was a type of unpadded glove worn by boxers. It was made of leather straps, often weighted with lead or iron.

[7]i.e., baptism.

on them or looking *forward to* them. After all, haven't we rescinded our baptismal pledge when we cease to bear witness to it?

Do we have to ask the pagans themselves about this? Let them tell us whether it is right for Christians to attend the shows. Why, the rejection of these amusements is the primary sign to them that a man has adopted the Christian faith. Therefore, if anyone shoves aside the distinctive badge of faith, he is plainly guilty of denying this faith. And what hope is there for a man who does that? When someone deserts to the enemy's camp, he throws down his arms, and he abandons the insignia and the oath of allegiance to his chief. He casts his lot—for life or death—with his new friends.

Evil Company Corrupts Good Habits

25. When a person is seated in a place that is totally devoid of God, will he be thinking of his Maker? When there is excited strife there for a charioteer, will there be peace in his soul? When he is caught up in the frenzied excitement, will he learn to be modest?[n]

For the sparks of passion are incited by such close association. For there is the intermingling of emotions. And there are the agreements and disagreements of the fans among themselves as they give their cheers. There is hardly any other reason that people go to the shows except to see and to be seen.

When a tragic actor is giving his speech, will a person be thinking about prophetic appeals? During the movements of the effeminate actor, will the spectator be meditating on a psalm? When the athletes are struggling hard, will he be ready to testify that there must be no striking of others again? Will he be moved with compassion when he is staring at the attacks of bears and the nets of the net fighters?

May God keep his people from passionate enjoyment of such cruel entertainment! How monstrous it is to go from God's church to the devil's church! From the sky to the pigsty, as they say. And how monstrous it is to raise your hands to God and then to wear them out applauding an actor. How monstrous it is to shout approval to a gladiator with the same mouth with which you said "Amen" over that which was holy! How monstrous it is to exclaim "Forever!"[8] to anyone else but God and Christ.

---

[8]Spectators shouted "Forever!" to the players with whom they were pleased.

6

What Fellowship Does Light Have With Darkness?

26. Furthermore, don't those who enter into the temptations of the shows open themselves up to evil spirits? I know of one instance—the Lord himself is a witness—of a woman who went to the theater and came back possessed. In the course of casting out the demon, the unclean creature was rebuked for daring to attack a believer. He replied, "In all truth I did it most righteously, for I found her in my domain."

Another case is well known, involving a woman who had been to hear a tragic actor. That night in her sleep, she saw a linen cloth[1], accompanied by a voice that strongly censured the actor's name. Five days later, the woman died. How many other clear proofs have we had of persons who fell from the Lord because of keeping company with the devil in the shows. No one can serve two masters. (Matt. 6:24) What fellowship does light have with darkness, or life with death? (2 Cor. 6:14)

---

[1]Perhaps, a burial shroud.

The Shows Stir Up Persecution

27. If for no other reason, we ought to abhor these pagan meetings and assemblies simply because God's name is blasphemed there. Or, because it is there that the cry, "To the lions!" is daily raised against us. Or, because decrees of persecution, as well as temptations, often issue forth from there.

What would you do if you were caught in that surging tide of ungodly judgments? Not that you would be in danger of harm from *men*, for nobody there knows you are a Christian. Rather, think how it must fare for you in heaven! When the devil is wreaking havoc on the church, do you doubt that the angels are looking down from above? Do you doubt that they are marking every man who speaks or listens to the blaspheming word? That is, the one who lends either his tongue or his ears to the service of Satan against God? Should you not, then, shun those benches where the enemies of Christ assemble? Should you not shun that seat of all that is harmful? Should you not shun that atmosphere that overhangs it all—an atmosphere defiled with wicked cries?

I admit that at the shows there are also pleasant things, things that are agreeable and innocent in themselves. In fact, there are some things that are excellent. However, nobody prepares a poisoned concoction by mixing poison with *bitter* things, such as gall and hellebore.[2] Rather, they put the poison into relishes that are well seasoned and have the sweetest of tastes. Likewise, the devil mixes his deadly potion in with things of God that are most pleasant and acceptable. Therefore, you should recognize that everything at the shows that is courageous, noble, stentorian, melodious, or exquisite in taste is but a drop of honey inside a poisoned cake. Your realization of the dangers you incur from the attractions of the shows must be greater than your taste for their pleasures.

28. Let the *devil's* guests feast on those dainties. The place and time of the feast, as well as the one who invites, are all

[2]Hellebore is a flowering European plant with a poisonous root.

theirs. Our banquets and wedding festivities are yet to come. Just as they will not be able to sit down in fellowship with us, neither can we sit down in fellowship with them. In this regard, everyone has to take his turn. Presently, they have gladness, and we are troubled. As Jesus said, "The world will rejoice; you shall be sorrowful." (John 16:20) So let us mourn while the pagans are merry. In that way, in the day of their sorrow, we can rejoice. Otherwise, perhaps by sharing in their gladness now, we may also share in their grief later.

You are too much of a weakling, Christian, if you would have pleasure in this life as well as in the next. Or, should I say that you are a simpleton if you think that this life's pleasures are genuine pleasures. Even the [worldly] philosophers consider quietness and rest to be the real pleasures. They find their joy and entertainment in these things. They even glory in these things. In contrast, you long for the goal line, the stage, the dust, and the place of combat!

Please answer me this: "Cannot we, who die only with pleasure, live without earthly pleasure?" For what is our wish other than that of the apostle? That is, to leave the world and to be taken up into the fellowship of our Lord. (Phil. 1:23) You have your joys where you have your longings!

The Pleasures Of God

29. Nevertheless, perhaps your objective is still to spend this period of existence in enjoyments. Well, then, how are you so ungrateful as to not thankfully recognize the abundant and exquisite pleasures that God has bestowed on you? How can you consider these to be insufficient?

For what is more delightful than to have both God the Father and our Lord at peace with us? What is more delightful than the revelation of truth? Or, the confession of our errors? Or, the pardon of the innumerable sins of our past life? What greater pleasure is there than to have no taste for earthly pleasure? Or, to have contempt for all that the world can give? What greater pleasure is there than to have true liberty, a pure conscience, a contented life, and freedom from all fear of death?

What is more noble than to tread the gods of the nations under foot? To cast out evil spirits? To perform cures? To seek divine revealings? To live for God? These are the pleasures—these are the spectacles—that befit Christians. They are holy, everlasting, and free. View these as your circus games. Fix your eyes on the "race course" of the earth, on the gliding seasons. Reckon up the periods of time. Yearn for the goal line of the final consummation. Defend the assemblies of the churches. Jump up at the sound of God's signal.Be roused by the angel's trumpet. Glory in the palms of martyrdom.

If the literature of the dramas delight you, then appreciate that we have literature of our own in abundance: a wealth of poetic verses, writings, songs, and proverbs. Moreover, these are not merely fictitious, but are true. Instead of being tricks of art, they are plain realities. Are you attracted to fights and wrestlings? Well, we have no lack of these, and ours are not of insignificant account. Look! Chastity overcomes immorality. Faithfulness slays treachery. Compassion strikes cruelty. Modesty out-wrestles immodesty. These are the contests we have among ourselves. It is in these that we win our crowns. Would you desire blood, too? We even have that—the blood of Christ.

The Grand Spectacle Of God

30. What a spectacle is that fast-approaching coming of our Lord! He will come as Lord over all, highly exalted, triumphant. Think of the praise of the angelic hosts! Think of the glory of the rising saints! Think of the kingdom of the just, thereafter! Think of the city of New Jerusalem![o]

What human judge or priest, in all his generosity, can bestow on you the privilege of seeing and exulting in such things as these? And yet even now, in a sense, we have them, through faith, by the visualization of the imagination.

What then are the things that eye has not seen, nor has ear heard? (1 Cor. 2:9) What are the things that have not even faintly dawned upon the human heart? Whatever they are, they are more noble, I believe, than any circus, theater, amphitheater, or track stadium!

On Prayer

1

The Lord's Prayer

1. Jesus Christ our Lord is the Spirit of God, the Word of God, and the Reason of God. That is, he is both the Word of reason and the Reason and Spirit of Word. And he has given to us, the disciples of the New Testament, a new form of prayer.[1] And in regards to this, it was necessary that new wine be stored in new wineskins and that a new piece [of cloth] be patched onto a new garment. (Matt. 9:16,17)

Besides, the practices of the past have all been modified. Some things, such as circumcision, have been changed. Other things, such as the rest of the Law, have been supplemented. Still others, such as prophecy, have been fulfilled. Finally, things like faith have been perfected. For the new grace of God has renewed all things from fleshly into spiritual. It has done this by superimposing on them the Gospel, which is the destroyer of the whole ancient system of the past.

In this Gospel, our Lord Jesus Christ has been approved as the Spirit of God, and the Word of God, and the Reason of God. He was mighty by the Spirit. He taught by the Word. And he came by the Reason. For that reason, Christ composed his Prayer in three parts.

Even John [the Baptist] had taught his disciples to pray vocally and in spirit. Prayer is enunciated by the voice, and it prevails only by spirit. However, everything John did was

---

[1] i.e., the Lord's Prayer.

done as a groundwork for Christ. When Christ had fully "increased," the whole work of the forerunner [John], together with his spirit itself, passed over to the Lord. This is just as John had predicted, saying it was necessary that Christ "should increase and [John] himself decrease." (John 3:30)

As a result, we no longer have in existence the exact form of words John taught others to pray. For earthly things have given way to heavenly. "He who is from the earth," said John, "speaks earthly things. And he who is here from the heavens speaks those things which he has seen." (John 3:31,32) And what comes from the Lord Christ that is not heavenly? This method of prayer certainly is!

Therefore, blessed brothers, let's consider his heavenly wisdom: First, there is his instruction to pray *secretly*. (Matt. 6:6) Through this command, he required faith on man's part. For we should be confident that Almighty God sees and hears beneath roofs—even into secret places. And he required humility in faith so that faith should offer its spiritual devotion to him alone. For faith believes that he sees and hears everywhere.[a]

The third stage of wisdom is this: we should not think that we must approach the Lord with a train of words. (Matt. 6:7,8) For we are certain that he looks after those who belong to him, without his having to be asked. And yet those brief words [of the Lord's Prayer] are supported on the substance of a great and blessed interpretation. For this Prayer is brief in words, but long in meaning. It embraces all of those things that need to be prayed about—whether it be veneration of God or the petitions on behalf of man. Not only that, it also embraces every sermon of the Lord, every record of his discipline. In short, the whole Gospel is epitomized in his Prayer.

"Our Father Who Is In The Heavens"

2. The prayer begins with a testimony to God and with the reward of faith. For we say, "Our Father who is in the heavens." In saying this, we not only address God, but we commend faith. For being able to call God "Father" is the

reward of faith. It is written, "To them who believed on him he gave power to be called sons of God." (John 1:12)

Our Lord very frequently proclaimed God as a Father to us. In fact he gave us the instructions to "call no one on earth father, but the Father whom we have in the heavens." (Matt. 23:9) In praying this way, we are thereby following his instructions. Happy indeed are those who recognize their father! In contrast, Israel is rebuked by those words to which the Spirit attests heaven and earth: "I have begotten sons, and they have not recognized me." (Isa. 1:2)

Furthermore, in saying, "Father," we are also calling him God. That title speaks of both filial duty and of power. Also, in addressing the Father, the Son is invoked too. For he said, "I and the Father are one." (John 10:30) And even our mother, the Church, is not passed by. For in the Father and the Son is recognized the mother, from whom arises the name both of Father and of Son. (John 17:20,21) In one broad term, or word, we honor God, together with those who belong to him, and we follow [Christ's] instructions. We also mark those who have forgotten their Father.[2]

"Hallowed Be Your Name"

3. The name of God, the Father, had not been proclaimed to anyone. Even Moses, who had asked him about his name, was told different names. (Ex. 3:13-16) However, to us it has been revealed in the Son, for the Son is now the Father's "New Name." "I have come," he said, "in the Father's name." (John 5:43) And again, "Father, glorify your name." (John 12:28) And even more plainly, "I have manifested your name to men." (John 17:6)

We pray, therefore, that this name "be hallowed." We don't mean this in the sense that we are wishing God well. As though there were anyone who could actually wish God well. Or as though He would suffer unless we wished Him well. However, it is plainly fitting for God to be *praised* in every place and time. We should praise him because of the

[2]i.e., the Jews.

memory of his benefits ever due from every man. So these words ["hallowed be your name"] serve as praise. After all, when is the name of God not "holy" or "hallowed" through himself? For he himself sanctifies all others. To him, the surrounding circle of angels never cease to say, "Holy, holy, holy." (Isa. 6:3)

In like manner, we also, who are candidates for angelhood, if we succeed in deserving it, start right here on earth to learn by heart that song that will hereafter be raised to God. We learn now the function of future glory. I'm speaking thus far of things for the glory of God. On the other hand, we are also praying on our own behalf when we say, "Hallowed be your name." For we are also asking that it may be hallowed *in us*, we who are in him. And we also ask on behalf of those for whom the grace of God is still waiting. Furthermore, in order to obey the commandment to "pray for all," we even ask this on behalf of our personal enemies. (1 Tim. 2:1; Matt. 5:44) For that reason, we do not say, "hallowed be it *in us*," but we say, "in all."

"Your Will Be Done"

4. According to this model, we next pray, "Your will be done in the heavens and on the earth." By this we don't mean that there is some power that prevents God's will from being done. We are not praying that he be able to successfully achieve his will. Instead, we are praying for his will to be done *in* everyone. In a figurative sense, *we* are "heaven" and "earth" in the sense that we are flesh and spirit.

Nevertheless, even if this phrase is to be understood literally, still the sense of the prayer is the same. We are still praying that God's will may be done on earth *in us*. And thereby it makes it possible for his will to be done in heaven.

And what is God's will other than that we should walk according to his discipline? (Ecc. 12:13) We are therefore praying that he supply us with the true meaning of his will, along with the ability to perform it. Thereby, we may be saved both in the heavens and on the earth. For the summation of his will is the salvation of those whom he has adopted.

Furthermore, there is that will of God that the Lord accomplished in preaching, in working, and in persevering. For he himself said that he did not do his own will, but that of the Father. Without a doubt, those things which he did were the Father's will. They were done as an example to us to preach, to work, and to persevere even unto death. And in order to accomplish these duties, we need the will of God.

In short, when we say, "Your will be done," we are actually wishing well *for ourselves*. For there is no evil in the will of God. This is true even though something other [than what we want] is imposed on us in proportion to what we deserve. So by this phrase, we are forewarning ourselves of the need for endurance. By his actual suffering in his own flesh, the Lord himself wished to demonstrate to us the infirmity of the flesh. So he said, "Father, remove this, your cup." But remembering himself, he added, "However, not my will but yours be done." (Luke 22:42) He himself *was* the Will and Power of the Father. (1 Cor. 1:24) And yet, to demonstrate the endurance that was needed, he gave himself up *to* the Father's will.

"Your Kingdom Come"

5. The phrase, "your kingdom come," is similar to that of "your will be done." Again, it is referring to the kingdom coming *in us*. For when does God ever *not* reign? After all, the heart of all kings is in his hand. (Pro. 21:1) But whatever we wish for ourselves we foretell for him. And what we expect *from* him, we attribute *to* him.

Since the manifestation of the Lord's kingdom is part of God's will and is something we anxiously await, why do some pray for this age [or world] to be extended? For, we pray that the kingdom of God may arrive, and it will bring about the end of the age [or world]. Our wish is that our reign may be hastened, not that our bondage be extended. Even if the Prayer had not called for us to pray for the coming of the kingdom, we would have sent forth that cry anyway, without being asked to. For that hastens to the realization of our hope. The souls of the martyrs, who are beneath the altar, cry in jealousy to the Lord, "How long, Lord, do you not avenge our blood on the inhabitants of the earth?" (Rev. 6:10) For, of course, their avenging is tied to the end of the age.

Nay, Lord, let your kingdom come with all speed. That is the prayer of Christians and the bewilderment of the pagans. It is the exultation of the angels. For the sake of it, we suffer; or rather, for the sake of it, we pray.

"Give Us This Day Our Daily Bread"

6. Notice how gracefully the Divine Wisdom[3] arranged the order of this Prayer. First, he addresses heavenly things—the name of God, the will of God, and the kingdom of God. It is only *after* these things that he includes room in the Prayer for earthly necessities. For the Lord had given the command, "Seek ye first the kingdom, and then even these shall be added." (Matt. 6:33)

Of course, we can interpret "give us this day our daily bread" *spiritually*. For Christ *is* our Bread. Christ is life, and bread is life. He said, "I am the Bread of Life." (John 6:35) And above that, "The Bread is the Word of the living God, who came down from the heavens." (John 6:33) We also find that his body is reckoned in bread: "This is my body." (Matt. 26:26) So in praying for "daily bread," we ask for eternity in Christ, and indivisibility from his body.

And even though those words can be understood in a physical sense as well, we must not do so to the exclusion of the religious remembrance of spiritual discipline. For the Lord commands that we pray simply for *bread*. That is the only food necessary for believers, because "all other things the *nations* seek after." (Matt. 6:32) Jesus inculcated this lesson [in his disciples] by examples, and he repeatedly taught it in his parables. For example, he said, "Does a father give his son a stone when he asks for *bread*?" (Matt. 7:9) He thus shows what it is that a son expects from his father. In fact, even the midnight caller asked [only] for *bread*. (Luke 11:5-9)

---

[3]i.e., Jesus. (1 Cor. 1:24)

Note that Jesus added, "Give us *this day...,*" in light of the fact he had previously said, "Take no careful thought about tomorrow, as to what you will eat." (Matt. 6:34) Addressing that theme, he gave the parable of the man who thought about enlarging his barns for his coming harvests, on the expectation of seasons of prolonged security. Yet, that very night he died. (Luke 12:16)

2

More On The Lord's Prayer

7. It was appropriate that after considering the generosity of God, we should next address his mercy. For what good is our daily bread if we are simply being fattened as a bull for slaughter? The Lord knew that he was the only One without guilt. For that reason he taught us to plead to have our debts forgiven. A prayer for pardon is actually a full confession. For he who begs for pardon fully admits his guilt.

And [the fact we are told to pray for forgiveness] demonstrates that repentance is acceptable to God. For he desires repentance rather than the death of the sinner. (Ex. 18:23) Moreover, in the Scriptures, debt signifies guilt.[b] And debt must be paid, unless such payment is forgiven. In the parable, the master forgave his slave's debt. (Matt. 18:21-35) The whole parable focuses on this point. However, that same servant, after being freed by his master, did not equally forgive the one who was indebted to him. As a result, he was indicted by his master and turned over to the tormentors to pay back the entire debt, down to the smallest coin. That is, he was to pay for every blameworthy thing, no matter how small.

This parable corresponds with our prayer: "as we forgive our debtors." In fact, in conformity with his prayer model, he had elsewhere said, "Forgive, and you shall be forgiven." (Luke 6:37) Likewise, when Peter asked whether forgiveness should be granted to a brother seven times, He said, "No, seventy-seven times." (Matt. 18:21,22) In this way, He reshaped the Law for the better. For in Genesis, *vengeance* was assigned seven times in the case of Cain, and seventy-seven times in the case of Lamech. (Gen. 4:15,24)

"Lead Us Not Into Temptation"

8. However, we should not simply pray about having our guilty acts forgiven. We must pray about avoiding such guilty acts altogether. So to complete this brief prayer, he added, "Lead us not into temptation." In other words, 'do not let us be led into it by him who does the tempting.' Far be the thought that the Lord would seem to tempt anyone. (Jas. 1:13) For that would mean that he was either ignorant of our faith or that he was eager to overthrow it. Weakness and evil are characteristics of the devil.

Even in the case of Abraham, God had commanded him to sacrifice his son [only] for the purpose of proving his faith, not for the sake of tempting him. God used Abraham as a living example of the commandment that God would later give: that man should love no one more than God. (Matt. 10:37) When tempted by the devil, he [Jesus] himself demonstrated who is the source and promoter of temptation. (Matt. 4:10) He confirmed this passage by later ones, saying, "Pray that you not be tempted." (Luke 22:40) However, they [the apostles] *were* tempted." They showed this by deserting their Lord. For they had fallen asleep instead of praying.

In fact, the final phrase of the Prayer harmonizes with this explanation. It interprets the meaning of "Lead us not into temptation" by saying, "but deliver us from the evil one."[1]

---

[1]It should be noted that Tertullian seems to know nothing of the phrase, "For thine is the kingdom and the power and the glory, forever, Amen." This is not surprising in light of the fact that the earliest manuscripts we have of Matthew do not contain this doxology either.

Summary Of The Lord's Prayer

9. In this small capsule of just a few words, think how many sayings of the prophets, the Gospels, and the apostles are touched on! Think also of how many sermons, examples, and parables of the Lord are touched on! Think of how many of our duties are addressed!

First, there is the honor of God in the word "Father." Then, there is the testimony of faith in the word "name." There is the offering of obedience in the word "will." There is the commemoration of hope in the word "kingdom." There is the petition for life in the word "bread." There is the full acknowledgment of debts in the plea that they be forgiven. And finally there is the anxious dread of temptation in the request for deliverance.

What wonder! Only God could teach us how he wished to be prayed to. The religious ordinance of prayer is therefore ordained by himself. It was living at the moment when it issued out of the Divine mouth, by his own Spirit. Prayer ascends by its own right into heaven, entrusting to the Father what the Son has taught.

Praying In Accord With Christ's Teachings

10. On another occasion, the Lord, who foresees human needs, after delivering his directive for prayer, said, "Ask, and you shall receive." (Matt. 7:7) So there are other prayers that are made according to the circumstances of each individual. So after beginning with the legitimate and customary prayers as a foundation, our additional needs have the right to be heard. They are, so to speak, a building constructed on the foundation of the customary prayers. Yet, even these prayers must be offered in accord with the Master's commandments.

11. We are as close to the ears of God as we are to the commandments of God. Remembrance of his commandments is what paves a way to heaven for our prayers. The most important commandment [concerning prayer] is that we do not go up to God's altar before we have resolved any

conflict with, or offense against, our brothers. (Matt. 5:22,23) After all, how much sense does it make to approach the peace of God without [our own] peace? How can you ask for the forgiveness of debts while you are unforgiving of others? How can we appease the father if we are angry with our brother? For, from the very beginning, all anger was forbidden to us. (Matt. 5:21,22)

Even Joseph, when he sent his brothers to fetch their father, told them, "Do not be angry in the way." (Gen. 14:24 LXX) Elsewhere [in Scripture], our rule of life is called "The Way." (Acts 9:2) So even back then, Joseph warned us, when set in the way of prayer, to not go to our Father with anger.[2]

In addition to that, the Lord expanded the Law by adding a prohibition against *anger* to the [existing] prohibition against murder. He does not even permit anger to be vented by an evil word. (Matt. 5:21,22) And even if we are compelled to anger, we must not remain angry beyond sunset, as the apostle instructed. (Eph. 4:26) How reckless it is to spend a day without prayer because you refuse to make satisfaction to your brother! Or else, to *lose* your prayer because of remaining angry.

12. Prayer must not only be free from anger, but it must also be free from all mental agitation. It must be uttered from a spirit that is like the Spirit to whom it is sent. For a defiled spirit cannot be acknowledged by a *holy* Spirit. Nor can a sad spirit be acknowledged by a joyful Spirit, nor a spirit in bondage by One that is free. Nobody grants entrance to his enemy. No, rather he gives entrance only to his comrade.

---

[2]Tertullian's argument here is quite typical of the thought patterns of the Jews and Christians of the early centuries. Joseph told his brothers to not be angry *in the way*. Tertullian sees in this a message to us since Christianity is called *The Way*.

3

Prayer Customs

13. What point is there in praying with hands that are washed, but a spirit that is soiled.[1] It is *spiritual* purities that are necessary if we are to "lift up holy hands" [in prayer]. (1 Tim. 2:8) Such hands must be pure from falsehood, murder, cruelty, sorceries, idolatry, and all other blemishes. These blemishes are conceived by our spirit, but are carried out by our hands. It is from *those* things that we must be purified—not the things that most people are superstitiously careful about. For they take water at every prayer,[2] even when they are coming from a bath of the whole body.

I investigated this custom carefully and thoroughly, searching for the reason behind it. In doing so, I learned that it was actually a commemorative act, imitating what happened at the surrender of our Lord.[3] However, we *pray* to the Lord. We don't *surrender* him! In fact, we should want to do the opposite of what the one who surrendered Jesus did. In other words, we should *refrain* from washing our hands. Unless that is, our hands have been soiled in the ordinary course of human ac-

---

[1]Apparently, many Christians in Tertullian's area washed their hands before prayer. It is not certain how widespread this custom was, nor when it originated. Perhaps, some thought that lifting up *holy* hands in prayer meant to lift up *clean* hands. Or, as Tertullian surmises, it may have been done in imitation of Pontius Pilate washing his hands.

[2]i.e., washing their hands before every prayer.

[3]i.e., Pontius Pilate washed his hands before handing Jesus over to be crucified.

tivities. Otherwise, they are clean enough, for we once washed them, along with the rest of our entire bodies, in Christ.[4]

14. Although the nation of Israel daily washed all its limbs, yet it is never clean. In all events, its hands are ever unclean, eternally dyed with the blood of the prophets and of the Lord himself. They [the Jews] are hereditary culprits to their fathers' crimes. (Matt. 23:31) For that reason they do not even dare to raise [their hands] to the Lord, out of fear that some Isaiah should cry out or that Christ should utterly shudder. We, however, not only raise our hands, but we even extend them. We take our model from the Lord's suffering [on the cross], so that even in prayer we confess to Christ.[5]

15. Since I have discussed one special point of empty observance,[6] it should not be too bothersome for me to set my brand against some other observances that may deservedly be called vain. By vain, I mean those customs that are followed without the authority of any instruction from either the Lord or the apostles. Such practices belong to superstition, not religion. For they are deliberate and forced. They are odd, rather than rational, practices. Such things should be restrained, if for no other reason, on the grounds that they put us on the same level as the Gentiles.[7]

Removing Cloaks Before Prayer

An example of this type of practice is the custom that some persons have of removing their cloaks when praying. You should note that the people of the nations do the same thing when approaching their idols. If this were a fitting practice, then the apostles would have included it in their instructions, since they taught concerning the prayer *garment*.[8] Unless of course,

---

[4]i.e., in baptism.

[5]The early Christians prayed with their arms outstretched, with palms turned upward, in imitation of Jesus on the cross.

[6]i.e., washing the hands.

[7]Christians thought of themselves as spiritual Jews, and so they referred to pagans as "Gentiles."

[8]i.e., the prayer veil. (1 Cor. 11:3-16)

someone wants to think that Paul left his cloak with Carpus during prayer! (2 Tim. 4:13)

How could it possibly be true that God does not hear those who pray with their cloaks on? He plainly heard the three saints in the furnace of the Babylonian king. Yet, they prayed with their trousers and turbans on. (Dan. 3:21)

Sitting After Praying

16. Another custom some have is sitting after prayer is ended. I see no reason for this practice, other than that which children give.[9] For what if that certain Hermas, whose writing is generally entitled *The Shepherd*, had not sat down on his bed when he was finished praying? What if he had done something else? Would we make a religious observance out of that too? Of course not.

In fact, even as it is written, the sentence simply says, "When I had prayed, and had sat down on my bed...." Obviously, this is merely said to describe the sequence of the narration. It is not said as a model for discipline. If it were, then we could not pray anywhere else except where there is a bed. So whoever sits in a chair or on a bench is acting contrary to that written work.

Furthermore, the nations have a similar practice. For they sit down after worshipping their petty images. So for that reason alone, we should avoid the practice, since it is a practice followed in the worship of idols.

Finally, this custom should be objected to on the grounds that it is *irreverent*. If the nations had any sense, they would recognize this too. We humans consider it irreverent to sit under the eye, and over against the eye, of someone we highly respect and venerate.[10] So how much more so is such a thing most irreverent under the eye of the living God. [Why

---

[9]i.e., children do things simply out of imitation of others. In this case, some Christians were imitating a certain passage from Hermas' *The Shepherd*, an orthodox early Christian work that many churches included in their canon of Scripture. In this passage, Hermas sat down on his bed after praying.

[10]It was considered a mark of respect to either stand, or prostrate oneself, when in the presence of one deserving respect.

should we sit] while the angel of prayer is still *standing* by? (Luke 1:11) Unless we are complaining to God that praying has worn us out!

Raising The Hands

17. We entrust our prayers to God more effectively when we pray with modesty and humility. That is, with not even our hands raised too high. Rather, we should raise them moderately and becomingly. And even our face should not be uplifted too boldly. For the tax collector [of Jesus' parable] prayed with humility. He was downcast, not only in his prayer, but in his head as well. Yet, he went away "more justified" than the self-righteous Pharisee. (Luke 18:9-14)

Likewise, the volume of our voices should be subdued. Just think how large our windpipes would have to be if God could only hear us because of the *noise* we make! But God hears the heart, not the voice. For he is the inspector of the heart. Even the demon of the Pythian oracle[11] said, "I understand the mute, and I plainly hear the speechless one." That being the case, do the ears of *God himself* have to wait for sound?

If they did, how could Jonah's prayer have found its way to heaven? For it had to worm its way out of the depths of the whale's stomach, through the entrails of so huge a beast. And then it had to go from the depths of the ocean through so great a mass of sea. So what possible advantage will they have who pray too loudly, other than to annoy their neighbors? Furthermore, by making their prayers audible, how are they any less guilty of error than if they were to pray in public?[12]

Withholding The Holy Kiss

18. Another custom has now become prevalent: those who are fasting withhold the kiss of peace—the seal of prayer—

---

[11]i.e., the oracle, or prophetess, of Delphi.

[12]Jesus instructed us to not pray in public. (Matt. 6:5,6)

after praying with the brethren.[13] Yet, when is peace more appropriately sealed with brothers than at such times? For our prayer ascends [to heaven] with more acceptability at the times of some religious observance.[14] In fact, this may encourage our brothers to share in our observance themselves.[c]

What prayer is complete if separated from the holy kiss? (Rom. 16:16) If a person is rendering [special] service to the Lord, how will peace hinder him? What kind of sacrifice is it that men depart from without peace? (Matt. 5:23,24) No matter how well we may pray, such prayer is not better than obeying the commandment given that we fast in secret. (Matt. 6:16-18; 1 Sam. 15:22) When we abstain from the kiss, everyone knows we are fasting. Even if there were some reason for this practice [of withholding the kiss], a person should follow the practice only at home. Otherwise, he will be disobeying [Jesus'] commandment. Of course, at home, it usually isn't possible to keep a fast entirely secret.

But wherever else you are able conceal your fast, you should do so in remembrance of the commandment. In that manner, you can satisfy the requirements of [Christ's] discipline when in public. At home, you can satisfy the requirements of this custom.[15] However, on the day of the Passover,[16] when the church in general is observing a fast—in a sense, a public fast—we do not transgress by withholding the kiss. For, in that instance, we do not need to conceal the fact that we are fasting, since we are all doing it in common.

---

[13]Paul told Christians that they were to greet each other with a holy kiss, a practice that was universally practiced in the early church, often at the conclusion of prayer. However, some were refraining from giving the holy kiss during periods when they were fasting.

[14]by the terms, "religious observance" and "rendering service," Tertullian is referring to things such as fasting.

[15]i.e., of withholding the kiss of peace.

[16]What is generally known today as Good Friday was called "Passover" by the early Christians. The term "Passover" was also used to describe the entire period from Good Friday to Pentecost, although Tertullian does not seem to be using it in that sense here.

The Stations

19. Let me now touch on the station days.[17] Most seem to think that during such days they must not be present at the sacrificial prayers. The reason given is that the station must be ended by receiving the Lord's body.[18] But does the Eucharist cancel a service devoted to God? Rather doesn't it bind the service more to God? Won't your station be more solemn if you have stood at God's altar? When the Lord's body has been received and reserved, each point has been secured—participation in the sacrifice and performance of duty.

The term "station" has perhaps received its name from the example of military life, for we are God's soldiers. (2 Tim. 2:1) If that is so, we should note that soldiers are not relieved of the duty of manning their stations just because there is rejoicing or sadness in the camp. Joy merely enables discipline to be carried out more willingly. Sadness causes it to be carried out more carefully.

Women's Apparel

20. Moving on to women's apparel, we find there is a variety of customs.[d] It would be presumptuous to address this subject the way that most holy apostle did.[19] However, it is not presumptuous to treat the subject *in accordance* with the apostle. In fact, the instructions of Peter on modesty of dress and ornamentation are quite plain as well. He said the same things as Paul because they both had the same Spirit. He likewise prohibited the glory of apparel, the pride of gold,

---

[17]By the term "station days," Tertullian is apparently referring to special days of fasting. The term "stations" goes back to the very early years of the church. The term may have originated as a metaphor to military guard stations. As such, it was usually used to refer to special prayer times throughout the day. Tertullian uses it in the latter sense elsewhere in this same tract.

[18]i.e., taking the Eucharist, or communion.

[19]i.e., Paul. "I desire...in like manner also, that the women adorn themselves in modest apparel, with propriety and moderation, not with braided hair or gold or pearls or costly clothing." (1 Tim. 2:8-10) (NKJV)

and the showy and elaborate arranging of the hair. (1 Pet. 3:1-6)

Woman's Prayer Covering

21. I now need to address the matter that is only haphazardly observed throughout the churches. I'm speaking of the issue of whether or not virgins should be veiled.[20] Those who grant virgins immunity from covering their heads argue that the apostle did not specifically mention "virgins." He only said that "women" were to be veiled.[21]

They argue that the apostle did not say "females," thereby addressing the feminine sex in general. Instead, he addressed only a certain type of female by saying "women." If he had used the word "females" instead, he would have made this rule absolute for every [type of] woman. However, since he named only one type of the [female] sex, he excluded the other classes by his silence. In conclusion, they say that he could have either specifically mentioned virgins or else used the term "female" so as to include virgins as well.

22. [Tertullian answers this argument at length in chapter 22 of his tract. His answer is essentially a summary of the arguments he develops in more detail in another tract, *The Veiling Of Virgins,* which is included in this volume. Rather than to duplicate the same arguments here, we have moved chapter 22 of Tertullian's tract to the appendix.[e]]

Kneeling

23. When it comes to the subject of kneeling during prayer, there is again a diversity of practice. I say this because there are a few persons who abstain from kneeling on the Sab-

---

[20]All married women in the early church wore the prayer veil in accord with Paul's commandment (1 Cor. 11:3-16). However, some churches interpreted Paul's commandment to not apply to virgins. The issue of whether virgins should be veiled is discussed in detail in Tertullian's tract *On The Veiling Of Virgins,* which is included in our anthology.

[21]The Greek term *gyne* can mean "woman," "married woman," or "wife," depending on the context.

bath.[22] Since this dissident practice[23] is on trial before the churches, hopefully the Lord will give his grace so that the dissidents will yield on this matter. Or else, that they will indulge their viewpoint in a way so as to not offend others.

We, however, have received the following practice: We abstain from kneeling only on the day of the Lord's Resurrection.[24] In fact, not only should we avoid kneeling, but also every other solicitous posture and function. We should postpone even our businesses, lest we give any place to the devil. Similarly, we distinguish the period of Pentecost[25] by the same ceremony of exultation.

But who would hesitate to prostrate himself every day before God during that first prayer with which we enter into the new day? During fasts and stations, no prayer should be made without kneeling, and without the other customary marks of humility. For at those times, we are not only praying, but we are also *pleading*, and making satisfaction to God our Lord.

---

[22]Tertullian is talking about the Jewish Sabbath (Saturday), not the Lord's day (Sunday). Perhaps the "dissidents" he is referring to are Jewish Christians.

[23]i.e., not kneeling during prayer on the Sabbath.

[24]The "day of the Lord's Resurrection" could refer either to Sunday or to Easter. However, it appears certain that in the present instance it means Sunday. For, in his tract, *The Chaplet*, Tertullian wrote, "We count fasting or kneeling in worship on the Lord's day to be unlawful. We rejoice in the same privilege also from Easter to Pentecost." (Chap. 3) The reason for this church-wide custom was that the Lord's day was a day for rejoicing.

[25]i.e., the period from Easter through Pentecost.

4

Pray Without Ceasing

As to specific *times* of prayer, nothing at all has been commanded, other than "to pray at every time and every place." (Eph. 6:18)

24. But how are we to pray "in every place" when we are forbidden to pray in public? (Matt. 6:5,6) When he said, "in every place," he meant that we are to pray at every opportunity and at every necessity that has been rendered suitable. For example, notice the praying that was done by those certain apostles.[1] They "began praying and singing to God" while in jail, in the presence of other prisoners. (Acts 16:25) Yet, this was not considered to have been a violation of the commandment.[2] Nor was it considered a violation when Paul prayed on the ship in the presence of all, when he "made thanksgiving to God." (Acts 27:35)

When To Pray

25. However, as for the *time* to pray, the outward observance of certain hours can be profitable. By that, I mean the common hours that mark the intervals of the day—the third, the sixth, and the ninth.[3] In the Scriptures, these times seem

---

[1]Paul and Silas.

[2]i.e., the commandment not to pray in public (Matt. 6:5,6).

[3]i.e., 9:00 a.m., 12:00 noon, and 3:00 p.m.. These were often referred to as the prayer stations, a custom that dates at least as far back as the early years of the second century.

to have been more solemn than others. For example, the first infusion of the Holy Spirit into the congregated disciples took place at "the third hour." (Acts. 2:1-4,14,15) Another example is Peter's praying on the day on which he experienced the vision of every sort of common thing displayed in that comparatively small vessel.[4] He went up into the upper chambers of the house for the purpose of prayer "at the sixth hour." (Acts 10:9) This same apostle was going into the temple with John "at the ninth hour," when he cured the paralyzed man.[5] (Acts 3:1)

Of course, these practices stand by themselves, without any *commandment* that they must be observed. Still, establishing a definite presumption about these [prayer times] is admittedly a good thing.[6] First, it adds discipline to the admonition to pray. And secondly, as if it were a regulation, it tears us away from our daily affairs to the duty of prayer. So after the pattern of what we read to have been Daniel's custom, which was in accordance with Israel's discipline, we pray at least three times per day. (Dan. 6:10; Ps. 55:17) For we are debtors to the Three: Father, Son, and Holy Spirit. Of course, the three times I mention are *in addition* to our regular prayers that are naturally due—without any exhortation—at the beginning and end of each day. It is also appropriate for believers to pray before taking food or going to the baths. For the refreshment and nourishment of the spirit should come before the refreshment and nourishment of the flesh. And heavenly things should precede earthly things.

Praying For Visitors

26. Of course, you will never bid farewell to a brother who has entered your house without a prayer. For the Scripture says, 'Have you seen a brother? You have seen

[4]This is a reference to Peter's vision of the unclean animals.

[5]The Scripture says, "Now Peter and John went up together into the temple at the *hour of prayer*, being the ninth hour."

[6]In other words, Tertullian is saying, "There is no commandment to pray at those specified times. But we can infer from Scripture that the apostles had a custom of praying at those times, and to follow such a custom is a good thing."

your Lord.'[7] This is especially true if the visitor is a stranger. For he might perhaps be an angel. (Heb. 13:2) Furthermore, when *you* are a guest of one of the brothers, you will surely not partake of earthly refreshments prior to heavenly. Otherwise, your faith will immediately be judged. How else will you obey the teaching to say, "Peace to this house" unless you exchange mutual peace with those who are in the house? (Luke 10:5)

27. Those who are more diligent in prayer are accustomed to add to the end of their prayers the "Hallelujah" or similar psalms.[8] And at the close of these, the company respond. And of course every prayer custom is excellent if it extols and honors God. For such things aim to unitedly bring Him enriched prayer, as though bringing to Him a choice sacrificial victim.

The Sacrifice Of Prayer

28. For this is the spiritual sacrifice that has abolished the sacrifices of former times. He says, "For what purpose do you bring me the multitude of your sacrifices? I have had enough burnt offerings of rams, and I do not desire the fat of rams and the blood of bulls and goats. For who has required these things from your hands?" (Isa. 1:11)

The thing that God *has* required is taught in the Gospel: "The hour will come," he said, "when the true worshippers will worship the Father in spirit and truth. For God is a Spirit, and he therefore requires his worshippers to be likewise." (John 4:23,24) We are the true worshippers and the true priests. Praying in spirit, we make a sacrifice of prayer, in spirit. This is indeed a proper and acceptable sacrifice to God. It is what he has required, and he looks forward to it for himself. This sacrificial offering [of prayer] is devoted from the whole heart. It is fed on faith and tended by truth. It is complete in innocence, pure in chastity, and decorated with

---

[7]Tertullian is probably referring to Matt. 25:40, "Inasmuch as you did it to one of the least of these My brethren, you did it to Me." (NKJV)

[8]This may be a reference to the last five psalms, sometimes known as "the great Hallelujah."

the garland of love. We should escort this sacrifice to God's altar with a procession of good works and with psalms and hymns. For it obtains all things for us from God.

The Contrast Between Old And New Testament Prayers

29. What has God ever denied to prayer coming from "spirit and truth?" And this is the type of prayer he requires. Think of how many examples there are of the effectiveness of prayer! We read of them, hear of them, and *believe* them.

Of course, the prayers of the old order [before Christ] delivered men from fires, beasts, and famines. Yet, such prayer had not received its form from Christ. How much greater, then, is Christian prayer! True, it doesn't bring the 'angel of dew'[9] in the midst of fire. And it doesn't muzzle lions or miraculously multiply the farmer's food for the hungry.[10] It has no delegated grace to avert any sense of suffering. Yet, it *does* give the ability to endure suffering, hurting, and grieving. It amplifies grace through virtue, so that faith will know what it receives from the Lord. That is, it enables us to understand *why* we suffer for the sake of God's name.

In the past, prayers used to call down plagues, scatter the enemy armies, and hold back rain. In contrast, now the prayer of righteousness *averts* all of God's anger. Our prayers keep watch *for the benefit* of personal enemies, and it prays *on behalf of* persecutors. In times of old, prayer brought down fire from heaven. (2 Kings 1:9-14) Now, it brings down *rain* from heaven.

Prayer is the only thing that "conquers" God.[11] But Christ has willed that prayer never be used for evil. All the power

[9]The angel who preserved the three Israelite youths in the fiery furnace, who were sprinkled, as it were, with dew.

[10]Apparently, a reference to the farmer whose food was miraculously multiplied to feed the disciples of Elisha. (2 Kings 4:42-44)

[11]No doubt a reference to Matt. 11:12: "And from the days of John the Baptist until now the kingdom of heaven suffers violence, and the violent take it by force." As Clement of Alexandria put it, "For God delights in being conquered in such things." *Salvation of the Rich Man*, 21.

he has conferred on prayer is for the cause of good. So prayer only knows how to recall the souls of the departed from the very path of death, to transform the weak, to restore the sick, to free the demon-possessed, to open prison doors, and to untie the bonds of the innocent. Furthermore, it washes away faults and repels temptations. It extinguishes persecutions. It consoles the low in spirit, and cheers those in good spirits. It escorts travelers, calms waves, and makes robbers stand aghast. It feeds the poor and governs the rich. It raises those who have fallen, stops others from falling, and strengthens those who are standing.

Prayer is the fortress of faith. It is the shield and weapon against the Foe who watches us on all sides. And so we never walk unarmed. By day, we are mindful of our stations.[12] At night, we remember our vigil. We guard the flag of our General by the weapon of prayer. In prayer, we await the angel's trumpet.

The angels also pray in a similar manner. (Heb. 1:6) In fact, every creature prays. Cattle and wild beasts pray and bend their knees. When they come forth from their corrals and dens, they look up to heaven with their mouths in motion.[f] Not only that, but the birds also rise out of their nests, raising themselves towards heaven. Instead of extending their hands, they expand their wings to form a cross. What they sing is like a prayer.[13]

What more can I say about prayer? Even the Lord himself prayed. And to him be the honor and virtue unto the ages of the ages!

---

[12]i.e., praying regularly on the third, sixth, and ninth hours.

[13]This beautiful passage calls to mind the teachings of St. Francis.

On The Apparel Of Women

Book Two

1

What Is Christian Modesty?

1. Handmaids of the living God, my fellow servants and sisters, I am emboldened to address a discourse to you because of the right of fellow-servantship and brotherhood I enjoy with you. I say this even though I am the lowest in that right of fellow-servantship. My discourse, of course, is not of affection but rather it paves the way for affection in the cause of your salvation.[1]

That salvation consists in exhibiting primarily the quality of modesty. I am speaking not only of the salvation of women, but of men also. For we are all "the temple of God" as a result of the dwelling of the Holy Spirit in us. (1 Cor. 3:16,17) Modesty is the keeper and the priestess of that temple. She is not to allow anything unclean or profane to come into it. Otherwise, the God who inhabits this temple might be offended, and he might forsake the polluted dwelling.

---

[1]The counsel given in this sermon is largely drawn from 1 Tim. 2:8-10: "Therefore, I desire...that the women adorn themselves in modest apparel, with propriety and moderation, not with braided hair or gold or pearls or costly clothing but, which is proper for women professing godliness, with good works;" and 1 Pet. 3:3: "Do not let your beauty be that outward adorning of arranging the hair, of wearing gold, or of putting on fine apparel, but let it be the hidden person of the heart, with the incorruptible ornament of a gentle and quiet spirit, which is very precious in the sight of God." (NKJV)

However, I am not going to speak about modesty per se. For the divine commandments that command and require modesty are quite sufficient, for they hedge us in on every side. Instead, I am going to talk about the matters that pertain to modesty. By that I mean the manner of life in which you should walk. I trust that God will permit me to make such public criticism. I do it, of course, with a view of criticizing my own life as well.

Most women have the daring to live as though modesty applies only to the bare chastity of the flesh, avoiding actual fornication. This is either a result of simple ignorance, or of pretension. They act as though there were no need for modesty in things external to the flesh, such as adornment and the arrangement of clothing, which are the studied qualities of form and brilliance.

They walk through life dressed in the same way as the women of the nations. Yet, a sense of *true* modesty is absent from such women of the nations. For there is nothing true in those who do not know God, the Guardian and Master of truth. It is plain that any modesty that does exist in Gentiles is imperfect and undisciplined.[a] It is so much so that it allows itself to degenerate into illicit extravagances of dress.

This is all in accord with the twisted morals of the Gentiles. For they crave after the very thing they try to avoid in action. How many of their women are there who do not eagerly desire to look pleasing to strangers? How many of their women do not carefully have themselves painted out for that very purpose. Yet, they then deny that they have been the object of someone's lust. This practice is in accord with one of the principles of Gentile "modesty": It is all right to *want* to sin, so long as you do not actually do so. Or even, not wanting to sin, but not quite refusing it. How incredible! As I said, everything that is not of God is twisted.

So take note! If you do not hold fast to goodness in its *entirety*, you will end up mingling evil with whatever good you may have. Just as you must turn aside from evil in all other things, so you must also do so in your walk. For you must be "perfect, as is your Father who is in the heavens." (Matt. 5:48)

Love Of Neighbor Requires Modesty

2. Perfect modesty is the same as Christian modesty. Under the standards of such a modesty, you not only do not desire others to have lust for you, you *detest* such lust.[b] Why would you want to excite lust toward yourself? If you profess to be a stranger to lust, why invite it?[c]

We ought to walk in such a holy manner, and with such a wealth of faith, that we can be confident and secure in our own conscience. We should desire that this gift[2] will abide in us to the end. Yet, we should not presume that it will. For he who presumes, has less fear. And he who has less fear, takes less precautions. And he who takes less precautions runs more risk. Fear is the foundation of salvation. (Pr. 9:10; Lk. 12:5) Yet, presumption is an impediment to fear.

So it is far better to be apprehensive that we may possibly fail than to presume that we cannot. For such apprehension will lead to fear. In turn, fear leads to caution, and caution to salvation. On the other hand, if we presume, there will be neither fear nor caution to save us. He who acts overconfidently, rather than warily, has no real security. On the other hand, he who is wary will have true security. May the Lord by his mercy take care that it may be lawful for his own servants to presume on his goodness!

But why do we become a source of danger to our neighbor? Why do we stir up lust in our neighbor?[d] I do not know whether God exempts from punishment someone who has been the cause of someone else's wrongdoing. For as soon as someone has lusted after your beauty, he perishes. (Matt. 5:28-30) For he has already mentally committed what he has lusted after. And you have become the sword that has slain him.

So although you are free yourself from the sin of lust, you are not free from the infamy attached to lust. For example, if someone is robbed while passing through another man's land, the owner of the land won't be charged with robbery.

---

[2]of salvation.

Yet, thereafter, the land is branded with infamy. And the infamy carries over to the owner of the land as well. Are we, then, going to paint ourselves up so that our neighbors may perish? If so, what happens to the command, "You shall love your neighbor as yourself?" (Matt. 19:19) Or, "Care not only for your own things, but for your neighbor's as well." (1 Cor. 10:24) No pronouncement of the Holy Spirit should be confined only to the immediate subject at hand. It should be applied and followed in every situation where its application is profitable.

In summary, both our own interests and those of others are at stake when we deliberately pursue outward beauty. Therefore, you should realize that it is not enough merely to reject the parade of artificial and enhanced beauty. Rather, even natural comeliness must be abrogated through concealment and indifference. For it too can be equally dangerous to those who see you.

Don't misunderstand me. Natural comeliness is not to be condemned. For it is a bodily joy—an additional outlay of the divine sculpture. It is a goodly garment of the soul. However, it is also to be feared. If for no other reason it should be feared because of the injuriousness and violence of suitors Even the father of the faith, Abraham, feared such things in regard to his wife's beauty. Isaac, too, falsely represented Rebecca as his sister. He thereby purchased his safety by an insult.[3]

What About Natural Beauty?

3. Now, [for the sake of argument] let it be granted that beauty is not to be feared. Let it be granted that it is neither troublesome to those who possess it nor destructive to those who desire it. And that it is not perilous to associates. Let it be thought that it is not exposed to temptations, nor surrounded by stumbling blocks. Still, it should be sufficient to say that it is not *necessary* to angels of God.[4]

---

[3]The "insult" being his denying that Rebecca was his wife.

[4]Apparently, by "angels of God," he means Christian women.

The reason is that, where modesty reigns, beauty is idle. Sensuality is the only real use of beauty. It is the fruit of beauty. Does someone really think there is some *other* fruitage for fleshly beauty to reap?[e] Yet, someone will no doubt say, "Well then, if sensuality is barred, and chastity is approved, can't we simply enjoy the praises of beauty by itself? Can't we glory in fleshly virtue?" Fine, then! Whoever receives pleasure from "glorying in the flesh," let him do so![f] (Gal. 6:13; 1 Cor. 3:21)

Without a doubt, a Christian *will* "glory" in the flesh. But it will be when his flesh has been mangled for Christ's sake—so that the spirit in it may be crowned. A Christian will not "glory in the flesh" in order to draw the eyes and sighs of young admirers. In short, to us, beauty is superfluous. If you don't have it, you can rightly disdain it. If you do have it, you can treat it as unimportant. However, if a holy woman is naturally beautiful, she should furnish no opportunity for the lust of others. If she is beautiful, rather than enhancing her beauty, she should cover it.

2

Christian Adornment Of The Face And Hair

4. As if I were speaking to Gentiles, addressing you with a Gentile precept that is common to all, I would say, "Yes, you are bound to please your husbands—but only your husbands."[1] And you will please your *husbands* only to the degree that you are not concerned about pleasing *others*.

Don't be concerned, blessed sisters. No wife is ugly in the eyes of her husband. She was sufficiently pleasing to him when he chose her. This is true regardless of whether she was commended by her appearance or her character. Let none of you think that if you quit beautifying yourselves you will incur the animosity and repulsion of your husbands.

Every husband expects *chastity*. A believing husband does not require physical beauty. For we are not captivated by the same charms that attract the Gentiles. On the other hand, an unbelieving husband will regard your adornment with suspicion because of the notorious rumors about us.[2] So for whom do you cherish your beauty? If it is for a believing husband, he does not require it. If it is for an unbeliever, he will be *suspicious* of it unless it is natural. So why are you

---

[1]Apparently, some Christian women were justifying their adornment on the grounds of wanting to please their husbands.

[2]It was rumored that the Christian "love feasts" were actually orgies.

eager to please either someone who is suspicious or someone who does not desire it?

5. Please don't misconstrue my suggestions. Please do not take them to an extreme and adopt an unkempt and disheveled appearance. I'm not suggesting that shabbiness and slovenliness are good qualities. Rather, I'm speaking of the appropriate amount of bodily arrangement. Simple and adequate refinements limit their desires. And there must be no overstepping of the line that is pleasing to God.

Cosmetics

Some women rub their skin with embellishments, stain their cheeks with rouge, and make their eyes prominent with black paint. Those who do so sin against God. Apparently, they are displeased with the creative skill of God! So with their own bodies, they criticize and indict the Artificer of all things! For when they change or add to his work, they are condemning Him.

And, of course, all of the things they add come from the opposing artificer. He, of course, is the devil. After all, who would show us how to change our bodies but he who through wickedness transformed man's spirit? No doubt he is the one who thought up such ingenious devices. He wanted you to openly wrong God in your very person. Whatever you are born with is the handiwork of God. So whatever is plastered on top of that is the work of the devil. How wrong it is to impose Satan's ingenuities on top of a work of God!

Our servants would never borrow something from our personal enemies, would they? Soldiers have no desire to receive something from the enemies of their own general, do they? In fact, it would be considered a wrongdoing to try to obtain something for your own use from the adversary of the one whom you serve. So, then, is it appropriate for a Christian to be assisted in *anything* by that evil one? If we accept his assistance, I'm not sure whether the name "Christian" still belongs to us. For we belong to the one whose teachings we eagerly desire to be instructed in. So [you should recognize] how alien the things of the devil are from *your* instruction and profession!

How unworthy of the Christian name it is to wear a falsified face! Particularly since every form of simplicity is imposed on us. (1 Tim. 2:9,10) Since lying with the tongue is not permitted, is it right to lie with your appearance? When we are commanded to not covet, is it right to seek after beauty that is not ours? When our schooling is in chastity, is it right to practice adultery in our outward appearance? Think about it, blessed sisters. How will you keep God's commandments if you are unwilling to keep your own person within his boundaries?

Dyeing The Hair

6. I notice that some women use saffron to change the color of their hair. They are ashamed of their own nationality—ashamed that they were not assigned to Germany or Gaul at the time of their conception.[3] So they try to change their nationality by changing their hair. Others concoct for themselves a flame-colored head. They think they are beautifying their head when they are really polluting it.

Furthermore, the strength of the dyes used actually burn and ruin their hair. In fact, the constant application of even a potion that is not drugged can be harmful for the scalp. For that matter, too much of the sun's heat is harmful. Yet, some seek it in order to give their hair a dry texture or to promote growth. How can grace be compatible with something injurious? How can [true] beauty be compatible with impurity?

Should a Christian woman heap saffron on her head, as though her head were an altar? For whatever is burned[4] to the honor of the unclean spirit is, in a sense, a sacrifice. Of course, I'm not talking about those things that are applied only for honest, necessary, and medical reasons.

---

[3]Saffron produces a yellow dye. The people of Germany and Gaul were generally blond-headed.

[4]A reference to the fact that dyes often burned the hair and scalp.

Furthermore, God said, "Who of you can make a white hair black, or a black one white?" (Matt. 5:36) So, in effect, some women refute the Lord! They say, "Look, we don't make our hair white or black—we make it *yellow*, which possesses more charm." Not only that, but those who regret having reached old age actually *do* attempt to change a white hair into black! What foolishness! The age that is the object of our wishes and prayers must blush for itself. For a type of thievery has been accomplished. They yearn for youth again, the time of our sinning. So they spoil the opportunity for the seriousness of maturity. May such folly be far from Wisdom's daughters!

Yet, the more someone tries to conceal old age, the more her age is detected. Here you already have a veritable eternity in the perennial youth of your head! However, we should await to put on true incorruptibility. I mean, the incorruptibility that awaits the Lord's new home for us, which the divine monarchy has promised. (1 Cor. 15:53; John 14:2,3) Yet, if it is so distasteful for you to approach the end of your own life, how are you going to hasten toward the Lord? How will you hasten to be rid of this wicked world?

Elaborate Hair Styles

7. All the labor that is spent arranging the hair—how does this help your salvation? Sometimes it is bound up; other times, it is loosed. Sometimes, it is cultivated; other times, it is thinned out. Why can't your hair simply be allowed to rest?

Some force their hair into curls; others let it hang loose and flying, but not with appropriate simplicity. On top of that, you affix all sorts of clever, woven wigs. Sometimes the wigs look like a leather helmet, as if they were a sort of a sheath for the head and a covering for the crown. Other times, wigs flow backwards towards the neck.

It's a wonder that there hasn't been open clamor against the Lord's teachings! Yet, it has been said that no one can add to his own height. (Matt. 6:27) You, however, do add some sort of curlers, or knobs, to your own *weight*, piling them upon your necks. If you feel no shame at this outrage, at least feel some for the accompanying pollution. Fear for the fact that you may be placing on a holy and Christian head the castoff hair of someone else's head. That is, a head that is perhaps unclean, sinful, and bound for Gehenna!

Your head is "free," so banish from it all of this slavery of adornment. In vain do you labor to look beautified. In vain do you enlist all the most skillful makers of false hair. God bids you to be veiled. (1 Cor. 11:2-16) Perhaps He does so out of fear that someone will see such heads!

And oh, most wretched as I am, may I only be allowed to elevate my head on that day of Christian rejoicing! Even if it is still below the level of your heels. Then I will see whether you will rise from the dead with your ceruse,[5] your rouge, and your saffron. Then I will see if you will rise in all your parade of headgear. Then I will see whether it will be women so adorned who will be carried by the angels to meet Christ in the air. (1 Thess. 4:13-17) If these adornments are something good in this life, if they are of God, they of course will be there along with the rising bodies. They will fit right in.

Yet, nothing can rise except flesh and spirit—alone and pure. Whatever, therefore, does not rise in the form of flesh and spirit is condemned. For it is not of God. You should abstain from things so condemned, even at the present time. Let God see you in this life as he will see you *then*.

Counsel To Men

Of course, it may seem that I, a man, am excluding women from their own domain out of envy. Yet, there are also things that should be disallowed to us men because of the serious demeanor we should have out of fear of God. (Phil. 4:8) As there is a defect of nature in women of wanting to be pleasing to men, so there is in men the same defect of wanting to please women.[6]

So our sex should likewise acknowledge the deceptive trickeries of appearance unique to us. For example, there is

---

[5]A cosmetic made from white lead.

[6]Tertullian is speaking about pleasing the opposite sex through our appearance.

the practice of cutting the beard too sharply. Or plucking it out here and there. Or shaving around about the mouth. Or arranging the hair in style, or disguising white hair with dyes. Or removing all of the fine hairs over the body. Or fixing each strand of hair in place with some womanly ointment. Or smoothing the skin all over with some type of abrasive powder or something. Or frequently looking into the mirror, gazing anxiously into it.

However, the knowledge of God has put an end to all desires to want to please others through luxuriant attraction. So these things are rejected as being frivolous and contrary to modesty. Where God is, modesty is there too. Seriousness is there as well, for it is the assistant and ally of modesty. For how can we practice modesty without seriousness—her instrument. Moreover, how will seriousness be able to aid modesty in her responsibility unless the entire man, including our appearance and countenance, is marked by seriousness?

3

How Should A Christian Dress?

9. Now, this necessary pruning away and retrenchment of excessive splendor applies equally well to the area of clothing. In fact it applies to all the remaining baggage of self-aggrandizement. After all, what good does it do to reflect moderation and honesty in your *face*—to have your face reflect a simplicity altogether worthy of the divine teaching—but to lavish all of the other parts of the body with the luxurious absurdities of splendor and finery?

Such splendor has an intimate connection with sensuality. And it clashes with modesty. These things are easily discernible from the fact that clothing is the tool often used to prostitute the grace of personal comeliness. In fact, without the vanity of lavish clothing, the grace of personal comeliness is viewed as useless and unappreciated, as though it were disarmed and broken. In contrast, when natural beauty fails, the supporting help of outward embellishment is seen as supplying a charm from its own inherent powers.

Our latter years of life are blessed with quietness at last. They are drawn into the harbor of modesty. Yet, the splendor and loftiness of clothing lure one away from that restful harbor. Through the seductions of desire, such clothing disturbs seriousness. For some, the provocative charms of clothing seem to compensate for the chill of [advanced] age.

Therefore, blessed sisters, take heed to not wear flashy and seductive clothing. However, there may be some of you under the demands of wealth, birth, or past dignities. These things may compel you to appear in public so gorgeously attired that it appears that you have not obtained [Christian] wisdom. Nevertheless, take heed to moderate an evil of this kind. Otherwise, perhaps under the *pretext* of necessity, you will give unbridled indulgence to an abuse of liberty.

How will you be able to fulfill the requirements of humility, which we profess, if you do not keep the enjoyment of your riches and elegances within bounds? For riches have the tendency to be very proud. And pride tends to exalt a person, rather than to humble him. Someone may ask, "Why, can't we use what belongs to us?" Well, who prohibits your using it? Yet, your use must be in accord with the apostle, who warns us, "Use this world as not abusing it; for the form of this world is passing away." (1 Cor. 7:29-31) He also tells us, "They who buy are to act as if they did not possess." Why? Because as he had explained, "The time is short."

For that matter, he plainly said that, due to the shortness of time, even those with wives should be as though they had none. (1 Cor. 7:29) With that in mind, what do you suppose his sentiments would be about these vain accessories? In fact, are there not many who do just what the apostle said? That is, they seal themselves up to be eunuchs for the sake of the kingdom of God.[1] (Matt. 19:12) They willingly relinquish a pleasure that is so honorable and, as we well know, permitted to us.

Are there not others who deny to themselves the very creations of God, abstaining from wine and meat? Of course, the enjoyment of wine and meat do not border upon any peril or concern. Still, through their disciplined use of food, those people make a sacrifice to God of the humility of their soul. Furthermore, before you received the knowledge of saving teachings, you who are wealthy used your riches and delicacies sufficiently. You enjoyed the fruits of your dowries.

---

[1]Tertullian is no doubt speaking figuratively of becoming eunuchs, and is probably referring to married couples who voluntarily lived celibate lives.

But we are the ones "upon whom the ends of the ages have come," having ended their course. (1 Cor. 10:11) We have been 'chosen by God before the world was' to arise in the extreme end of the times. (Eph. 1:4) And so we are trained by God for the purpose of chastising—or, so to speak, emasculating—the world. We are the 'circumcision of all things'—both spiritual and fleshly. (Phil. 3:3) For both in the spirit and in the flesh we circumcise worldly principles.

The Origin Of Dyes, Precious Metals, And Cosmetics

10. No doubt, of course, it was God who showed humans how to dye wool with the abstracts of herbs and the fluids from shells![2] When he was creating the universe, no doubt he forgot to issue the command to bring forth purple and scarlet sheep. No doubt it was God, too, who, after careful deliberation, devised the manufacture of those garments that are very light and thin in substance, but very heavy in price.

Oh, and it must have been God who created magnificent implements of gold for grooming and parting the hair. And, too, it was God who introduced the fashionable practice of piercing the ears. He delighted in seeing his own handiwork tormented. He delighted in seeing innocent babies tortured, learning to suffer with their earliest breaths. All of this was merely for the purpose of hanging some sort of precious stone from those bodily scars—scars born for the steel. And yet, as anyone can plainly see, the Parthians use those same stones as ornamentations on their *shoes*.

The glory of gold sweeps you away! Yet, a certain nation uses gold to make ordinary chains, or so Gentile literature tell us. None of these things [such as gold] are valued because of any intrinsic worth, but primarily because of their rarity. Furthermore, it was the sinful angels who taught men the art of working with these materials.[3] They also revealed to men

---

[2]Some dyes, such as purple, were extracted from certain mollusks. Tertullian is speaking sarcastically in this paragraph.

[3]According to the Book of Enoch, sinful angels came down to the earth in Noah's day and, among other things, taught humans the art of working with precious metals and gems. According to Enoch, they also taught women the use of cosmetics.

where these gems and precious metals could be found. So these substances became expensive for a couple of reasons in addition to their rarity. First, extensive labor was needed to work them. Secondly, they had been revealed by angels. And this costliness, in turn, excited a lust in women to possess them.[8]

Now, those same angels also instructed humans in the use of eye make-up and how to dye wool. Yet, as Enoch tells us, those angels were condemned by God. So how can we possibly please God while we revel in the use of the things those angels taught? For because of such things, those angels provoked the anger and vengeance of God.[4]

Why God Permits Temptations

Let me grant that God foresaw all these things and that he permitted them. Let me grant that Isaiah found no fault with the garments of purple, the scarfs, and the crescent-shaped neck ornaments. (Isa. 3:18) However, let us not delude ourselves, as the Gentiles do, into thinking that God is merely a Creator—and not also One who looks down on his own creatures.

For we will act far more profitably and cautiously if we hazard the presumption that God provided all of these things in the beginning and placed them in the world as a test to prove the discipline of his servants. For the freedom of use is perhaps the means by which God conducts an experimental trial to test our self-control.

Don't wise family heads purposely offer and permit certain things to their servants in order to test whether they will use the thing thus permitted? And to see *how* they will use

[4]The early Christians generally had a high regard for the Book of Enoch. In fact, under the inspiration of the Holy Spirit, Jude himself directly quoted from Enoch 1:9, "Now Enoch, the seventh from Adam, prophesied about these men also, saying, "Behold, the Lord comes with ten thousands of His saints to execute judgment on all, to convict all who are ungodly among them of all their ungodly deeds which they have committed in an ungodly way, and of all the harsh things which ungodly sinners have spoken against Him." However, after the time of Constantine, Christians began to disregard the Book of Enoch, particularly after it was attacked by Jerome and Augustine.

them. That is, will they use them honestly? Will they use them with moderation? Yet, how far more praiseworthy is the servant who abstains entirely. How far more praiseworthy is the servant who has a wholesome fear even of the *privileges* allowed by his lord. As the apostle said, "All things are lawful, but not all are expedient." (1 Cor. 10:23) How much more readily will we fear what is *unlawful* when we have a reverent awe of what is *lawful*?

4

The Testimony Of Our Attire

11. Furthermore, what reason do you have to appear in public in excessive grandeur? For you are removed from the occasions which call for such display. You do not make the rounds of the temples. You do not demand to be present at the public shows. And you do not have any dealings with the holy days of the Gentiles. Yet, it is for the sake of all these public gatherings that all the vain displays of dress are made before the public eye. There is much seeing and being seen. The Gentiles make showy displays to either transact voluptuous exchanges or to inflate their glory.

In contrast, you have no reason for appearing in public except for sober-minded things. (1 Tim. 5:13,14) Either some brother who is sick is visited. Or the sacrifice is offered. Or the word of God is administered. Whichever of these you choose is a holy and serious undertaking. It requires no extraordinary attire. It requires no careful adornment and unbridled looseness.

And if the requirements of Gentile friendships and of kindly offices call you, why not go forth clad in your own armor. In fact, you should do this all the more so since you are going to persons who are strangers to the faith. In this way, they can see a difference between the handmaids of God and those of the devil. Thus you will be an example to them, so that they can be edified in you. As the apostle said, "God may be magnified in your body." (Phil. 1:20) But he is magnified in the body only through modesty, and, of course, through clothing that is suitable to modesty.

However, some will argue, "But the name [Christian] will be blasphemed in us if we make any detracting change from our old style and our old clothing." Well, then, let's not abolish any of our old vices! If we must maintain the same appearance as before, let's maintain the same *character* as well. That way, the nations surely won't blaspheme!

Is it really a "grand blasphemy" when it is said, "Ever since she became a Christian, she walks in poorer clothing"? From the time [of your conversion] you have been made more wealthy.[1] So are you going to fear to *appear* poorer? Ever since that time, you have been made cleaner. So do you fear to *appear* to be more soiled? Should a Christian walk according to the principles of the Gentiles, or according to the principles of God?

Avoiding The Garb Of A Prostitute

12. Our only wish should be that there may never be a cause for *just* blasphemy! Aren't you more apt to cause blasphemy if you appear in public decked out and painted after the manner of the immodest? Particularly, since you are called the priestesses of modesty! Otherwise, how are you any different from the poor unhappy victims of the public lusts?[2] In times past, there were laws to restrain prostitutes from the use of marital and matronly decorations. Now, however, because the depravity of the age increases daily, the prostitutes have been raised nearly to an equality with all the most honorable women. As a result it is difficult to tell them apart.

The Scriptures themselves suggest to us that showy allurements of the body are invariably associated with—and appropriate to—bodily prostitution. That powerful city[3] that

[1] i.e., spiritually wealthy.

[2] i.e., the prostitutes.

[3] i.e., Babylon the Great.

presides over the seven mountains and over the many waters has deserved the name "prostitute" from the Lord. Notice what kind of clothing she is wearing that causes her to be compared to a prostitute. She sits "in purple and scarlet, with gold and precious stones." (Rev. 17:4) How foul are the things that are needed to accurately describe a foul prostitute!

Remember, too, that it was the fact that Tamar "painted up and adorned herself" that led Judah to regard her as a harlot. (Gen. 38: 14 LXX) Because her identity was hidden underneath her veil, and because her clothing made her appear to be a harlot, he judged her to be one. Accordingly, he addressed her and bargained with her as such. So here we have an additional confirmation of what I am saying: That we must take all steps necessary to prevent others from having any immodest association or suspicion of us.

Why should the integrity of a chaste mind be defiled by the suspicion of a neighbor. Why should someone desire in *me* something to which I am averse? Why doesn't my attire announce my character beforehand so that my ears will not hear shameless things that wound my spirit? To assume the appearance of a modest woman is permitted. To assume that of an immodest woman is not.

Let Your Light Shine

13. But perhaps some woman will say, "I don't care what wrong assumptions others may have about me. For I do not need the approval of humans. God is the inspector of the *heart*." We all know that is true. Still, we must remember what God said through the apostle: "Let your uprightness appear *before men*." (Phil. 4:5,8) And why should we let our uprightness appear before men? So that evil will have no access to us at all. So that we may be an example and witness against evil.

Why else was it said, "Let your works shine?" Why else did the Lord call us the "light of the world?" Why else did he compare us to a city built upon a mountain? (Matt. 5:14-16) Those words are not appropriate if we do not shine in the midst of darkness, if we don't stand tall among those who are sunk down. If you hide your lamp beneath a bushel basket, you will necessarily be left in the dark. Many will bump into you. It is our good works that make us luminaries of the world.

If something is truly and completely good, it does not love darkness. It rejoices in being seen. It exults over the fact that people point at it. As a Christian, it is not enough to simply be modest *inside*. Your modesty must be obvious to others as well. The magnitude of modesty should be so great that it flows from the mind to the garment. It bursts forth from the conscience to the outward appearance. So that even from the outside it may gaze upon its own dwelling—a dwelling suitable for faith to live in perpetually.

Delicate fineries tend to weaken the manliness of faith because of their softness and effeminacy. They should therefore be discarded. Otherwise, I fear that the wrist that has been used to being encircled with a leaf-like bracelet will not be able to endure the chain that makes the wrist numb and hard as iron. I wonder if the leg that has rejoiced in the anklet will allow itself to be squeezed into the shackles. I'm afraid that the neck that is adorned with pearl and emerald necklaces will give no room for the executioner's sword.

Therefore, blessed sisters, let us think about hardships *now*, so we will not feel them later. Let us abandon luxuries now, so later we won't miss them. Let us stand ready to endure every type of violence, having nothing to worry about leaving behind. For such things act as chains to impede our hope. If we desire heavenly ornaments, let us cast away earthly ones.

Do not love gold. For in this one substance are branded all of the sins of the people of Israel.[4] You ought to detest that which ruined the Jews, the thing that was adored by those who forsook God. Even then, gold was fitting food *for the fire*. In contrast, Christians have always—and now more than ever—passed their times in *iron*, not in gold.

---

[4]Perhaps a reference to the golden calf, the original idolatry of the Israelites.

The robes of martyrdom are now being prepared. The angels who are to carry us are now waiting in expectation. Go forth to them already arrayed in the "cosmetics" and "jewelry" of *prophets and apostles*: Obtain your whiteness from simplicity. Get your ruddy hue from the blush of modesty. Paint your eyes with meekness and your mouth with silence. Implant the words of God in your ears. Array your necks with the yoke of Christ. Submit your head to your husbands, and you will be adequately adorned.

If you busy yourselves with spinning and keep your feet at home, you will please your husbands more than by decking yourselves in gold. Clothe yourselves with the silk of uprightness, the fine linen of holiness, and the purple cloth of modesty. Adorned in this manner, you will have God as your Lover!

On Baptism

1

Heretics Scoff At Baptism

1. Happy is our sacred mystery[1] of water. For by washing away the sins of our early blindness, we are set free and admitted into eternal life. An essay on this subject is worthwhile. First, it will instruct those who are new in the faith. Secondly, it will teach those who have been content with merely believing.[2] Because of their ignorance, they have a probable faith that is untried. They have not made a full examination of the [Christian] traditions. As a consequence, a viper of the Cainite heresy, having recently become familiar in this region, has carried away a great number with her venomous doctrine.[3] She has made it her first aim to destroy baptism. This is quite fitting, because vipers, snakes, and lizards are generally attracted to arid and waterless places.

---

[1]The Latin word used by Tertullian here is *sacramentum*, which basically means a "guarantee" or "oath." *Sacramentum* was used by the Latin-speaking Christians as the equivalent of the Greek word *mysterion*, a term used frequently by Paul. *Mysteria* refer to the secret plans, provisions, and graces of God that have been revealed, or partly revealed, to Christians.

[2]That is, those who have bare faith, without a full understanding of sacred things.

[3]The Cainites were a gnostic sect that taught against water baptism. They believed that Cain, Esau, Judas, and the people of Sodom all had special divine knowledge hidden from most other humans. They circulated a spurious "Gospel of Judas."

However, we little fishes are born in water, after the example of our *Ichthys*[4] Jesus Christ. And we have safety in no other way than by permanently abiding in water. So that monstrous creature, who had no right to teach even sound doctrine[5], knew very well how to kill the little fishes—by taking them away from the water!

2. The perversity of her false doctrine is very great. It shakes the faith, and it can entirely block a person from receiving the faith. In fact, it opposes the faith on the very principles of which the faith consists! Absolutely nothing makes men's minds more hardened than the simplicity of the divine works which are visible in the *act* [of baptism]. Particularly, when this is compared with the grandeur promised in the *effect*. The resulting attainment of eternity is deemed unbelievable merely because the act is one of great simplicity—without pomp. For without any type of unusual preparation, a man is lowered in the water. With the utterance of a few words, he is dipped, and then rises again not much the [physically] cleaner.[6]

[a]Oh, miserable unbelief—to deny God his own properties, simplicity, and power! What then? Is it not wonderful, too, that death should be washed away by bathing?[b] Shouldn't we expect divine works to be above all wonder? We ourselves wonder, but it is *because* we believe. On the other hand, unbelief wonders, but does not believe. It wonders at the simple acts, as if they were futile. And it scoffs at the grand results, as if they were impossible. May it be just as you think. The divine declaration is sufficient to meet each point of argument: "God has elected the foolish things of the world

---

[4]The Greek word *ichthys* (fish) was an acrostic for "Jesus Christ, the Son of God, the Savior."

[5]The Scriptures forbid a woman to teach in church. (1 Cor. 14:34, 35; 1 Tim. 2:11, 12)

[6]In his work *De Corona,* Tertullian gives this description of baptism: "Right before we enter the water, in the presence of the congregation and under the hand of the president, we solemnly profess that we disown the devil, and his pomp, and his angels. Then we make a confession of faith that is somewhat more ample than the Lord has appointed in the Gospel, and we are immersed three times. Then, when we are taken up as new-born children, we first of all taste a mixture of milk and honey. And we refrain from the daily bath for a whole week." Tertullian *De Corona* chap. 3

to confound its wisdom." (1 Cor. 1:27) And again, "The things very difficult with men are easy with God."[c] (Luke 18:27)

Water: The Substance Of Mystery

3. Remembering that this declaration is a definite rule of conduct, we nevertheless proceed to answer the objection: "How foolish and impossible it is to be formed anew by water! Pray tell, in what respect has this material substance earned a position of such high dignity?"

So let's first examine the authority of this liquid element. This authority is well documented, even from the very beginning. Water is one of those things that was present with God in a shapeless state, even before the furnishing of the world. "In the first beginning," says Scripture, "God made the heaven and the earth. But the earth was invisible, and unorganized, and darkness was over the abyss. And the Spirit of the Lord was hovering over the waters." (Gen. 1:1-2) So the first thing which you have to respect is the antiquity of waters. Second, they have dignity, because they were the seat of the Divine Spirit. They were no doubt more pleasing to Him than all other elements that were then in existence. At that time, the darkness was complete and shapeless, without the ornament of stars. The abyss was gloomy, the earth was unfurnished, and the heaven was unformed. Only water supplied a worthy vehicle for God. For it has always been a perfect, joyful, simple, material substance—pure in itself.

Notice, too, the fact that waters were in some way the regulating powers by which God ordered the world. He suspended the heavenly firmament by "dividing the waters." He brought forth the dry land by "separating the waters." (Gen. 1:6-8) After the world had all been set in order, and was ready to be filled with inhabitants, the waters were the first to be commanded "to bring forth living creatures." So water was the first substance to produce living creatures. It is no wonder, then, that waters know how to give life in baptism.

In fact, wasn't the work of creating man himself also achieved with the aid of waters? To be sure, suitable material is found in the *earth,* but it is unsuitable unless it is moist and full of liquid.[d] I could continue to cite the proofs of the "authority" of water to show its great power and grace. Or the many ingenious devices, functions, and uses it supplies to the world. But I fear I may seem to have collected the praises of water rather than the reasons for baptism. Nevertheless, I would thereby teach more fully these things: God has dispersed water throughout all of his products and works. And, without a doubt, he has also made water obey him in his own special mysteries—so that this material substance which governs *earthly* life also acts as an agent of the *heavenly.*

2

The Procedure And Significance Of Baptism

4. By these points, then, I have demonstrated that primary principle of baptism: Just as the Spirit of God hovered over [the waters] in the beginning, so he would continue to linger over the waters of the baptized.[e] So a holy thing [the Spirit] hovered over a holy substance. Or, perhaps, the water borrowed holiness from [the Spirit] that hovered over it. It is necessary that in every case an underlying material substance should catch the quality of that which hovers over it.[f] So the nature of the waters, sanctified by the Holy One, conceived the power to sanctify.

Does Special Water Have To Be Used?

Let no one say, "Why then, pray tell, are we baptized with the very waters that existed in the first beginning?" Of course, it is not with those *same* waters, except that all types of water are of the same *genus*. However, the *species* of water are of various types. But the basic characteristics of the genus appear in each of the species of water. Accordingly, it makes no difference whether a man is washed in a sea, pool, stream, fountain, lake, or riverbed. Neither is there any distinction between those whom John baptized in the Jordan and those whom Peter baptized in the Tiber. Otherwise, the eunuch whom Philip baptized, while in the middle of his journeys, with whatever water happened to be available, might have derived less (or perhaps more) of salvation than others. (Acts 8:26-40)

Therefore, because of their pure origin, all waters attain the sacred [or sacramental] power of sanctification, after God's blessing is invoked. The Spirit immediately supervenes from the heavens and rests over the waters, sanctifying them through himself. Being sanctified, they thereby acquire the power to sanctify.

The Significance Of Baptism

To an extent, there is a spiritual parallel to the simple act: Since we are defiled by sins, as if by dirt, we should be washed from those stains in water. However, sins do not show themselves on our physical skin. For example, no one carries on his skin the spot of idolatry, or fornication, or fraud. Rather, persons of that kind are foul in the *spirit*, which is the author of the sin. After all, the spirit is lord; the flesh is merely the servant. Yet, they mutually share in the guilt: the spirit, because it commands; the flesh, because it serves the spirit. Therefore, after the waters have been given medicinal virtue through the intervention of the angel, then the spirit is bodily washed in the waters, and the flesh is likewise spiritually cleansed.

Pagan Baptism

5. But someone may object, "Even the nations, who are strangers to all understanding of spiritual powers, claim their idols imbue waters with the same effectiveness." So they do, but they cheat themselves by using waters that are widowed [i.e., that lack the Holy Spirit's presence]. But it's true that washing is the channel through which they are initiated into certain sacred rites—such as the notorious rites of Isis or Mithras. They also honor their gods by washings. Moreover, by carrying water around and sprinkling it, they everywhere purify country-seats, houses, temples, and

whole cities. They are baptized at all events like the Apollinarian and Eleusinian games. They presume that such baptisms bring about their regeneration and the remission of the penalties for their perjuries. Among the ancients, when a person committed murder, he would go in search of purifying waters.

In short, the very nature of water—its suitability for washing things—leads men to flatter themselves with a belief in omens of purification. That being the case, how much more will waters truly render that service through the authority of God, who created water. If men think that water is endowed with a medicinal virtue by religion, what religion is more effective than that of the living God? Acknowledging this, we also recognize here the zeal of the devil in imitating the things of God. (2 Cor. 11:14) So it is no surprise to find him, too, practicing baptism on his subjects. But what true similarity is there? Can the unclean cleanse? Can he who ruins set free! Can the damned pardon? Will the devil destroy his own work, by washing away the sins which he himself inspired? I say these things as testimony against those who reject the faith. Instead of putting their trust in the things of God, they trust in the imitations of God's rival.

There are other cases in which, without any sacred mystery, unclean spirits brood on waters in imitation of the way the Divine Spirit hovered in the very beginning. For example, look at all the shady fountains, secluded brooks, the pools in the baths, and the water ducts in private houses. Or notice the cisterns and wells that are said to have the property of "spiriting away" through the power of a harmful spirit. Men who have drowned or whom waters have affected with madness or fear are called nymph-struck or pixilated. Others are said to have hydrophobia.[1]

Angelic Presence At Baptism

Why have I cited these examples? For the benefit of some who may think it too hard to believe that a holy angel of God

[1]*Hydrophobia* means "fear of water."

should grant his presence to waters, to make them suitable for man's salvation. At the same time, the evil angel uses the same element [water] to man's ruin. If it sounds to you like a strange new thing for an angel to be present in waters, you should be aware that this very thing was previously foreshadowed. For an angel used to intervene and stir the pool at Bethsaida. (John 5:1-9) Those who were in ill health used to watch for him. Whoever was the first to descend into the waters after the angel's washing would be healed. This physical healing foreshadowed a spiritual healing. For, as a rule, fleshly things always precede and prefigure spiritual things. So when the grace of God advanced to higher degrees among men, a greater power was granted to the waters and to the angel.

Those angels who used to heal physical defects now heal the spirit. Those who used to bring about temporal health, now bring about eternal. Those angels who used to set free only once a year, now save people *daily*. For death is done away with by the washing of sins. When the guilt is removed, the penalty is, of course, also removed. So man will be restored into the "likeness" of God. In times past, man was merely conformed to the "image" of God. The "image" is considered [to be] in His form; the "likeness," in His eternity. For man receives again that Spirit of God which he had first received from God's breath, but which man had afterward lost through sin.

6. We do not obtain the Holy Spirit *in* the waters. But in the water, under the witness of the angel, we are cleansed, and prepared for the Holy Spirit. In this case also a pattern has come first, for John was the Lord's forerunner, "preparing his ways." (Luke 1:76; Isa. 40:3) In the same manner, the angel, the witness of baptism, "makes the paths straight" for the Holy Spirit, who is about to come upon us. This is done by the washing away of sins, which faith obtains, sealed in the Father, and the Son, and the Holy Spirit.

Through the benediction, we have these three [the Father, Son, and Holy Spirit] as the witnesses of our faith. We also have them as the sureties of our salvation. "In the mouth of three witnesses every word shall stand." (Deut. 19:15; Matthew 18:16) Accordingly, how much more is the number of the divine names sufficient for the assurance of our hope! After the pledging both of the testimony of faith and the promise of salvation under "three witnesses," the Church is, of necessity, mentioned.[2] For wherever there are three, (the Father, the Son, and the Holy Spirit,) there is the Church, which is a body of three. (Matt. 18:20)

Anointing With Oil

7. After this, when we have emerged from the bath, we are thoroughly anointed with a blessed oil. This is a practice derived from the ancient procedure. For ever since Aaron was anointed by Moses, men have been anointed with oil from a horn upon entering the priesthood. (Ex. 29:7; Lev. 8:12) So Aaron is called "Christ," [i. e. "Anointed"] from the anointing, which is the oil. The spiritual application is that this anointing furnished an appropriate name for the Lord, because he was anointed with the Spirit by God, the Father. It is written in the Acts, "For truly they were gathered together in this city against your holy Son whom you have anointed." (Acts 4:27) So in our case, also, the anointing oil runs on the *body*, but it profits us *spiritually*. Likewise, the act of baptism is physical, in that we are plunged in water, but the effect is spiritual, in that we are freed from sins.

Receiving The Holy Spirit

8. Next, the hand is laid on us, summoning and inviting the Holy Spirit through prayer. After all, through their human ingenuity, men are able to summon a breeze into water and, by the application of hands from above, they unite this wind into one body with another breeze of melodious sound.[3] If so, isn't it equally possible for God, in the case of his own musical organ [i.e., Man], to use "holy hands," to produce a beautiful new melody—one that is spiritual?[g]

---

[2]Early baptismal statements of faith, similar to the well-known Apostles Creed, usually contained the words, "I believe...in the holy church," or some equivalent expression.

[3]This reference is to an ancient musical water organ.

(1 Tim. 2:8) Then that Holiest Spirit willingly descends from the Father over our cleansed and blessed bodies. He rests over the waters of baptism, recognizing, so to speak, his primeval seat. (Gen. 1:2)

He glided down on the Lord "in the shape of a dove" so that the nature of the Holy Spirit might be declared through a creature of simplicity and innocence. For even in its bodily structure, the dove is without literal gall.[4] For that reason he says, "Be as simple as doves." (Matt. 10:16) Even this is not without the supporting evidence of a preceding pattern. The waters of the flood purged the ancient sin [of the world]. It was, so to speak, a baptism of the world. After this "baptism," a dove was the herald which announced to the earth the soothing of heavenly anger. She had been sent her way out of the ark, and had returned with the olive branch, a sign which even among the nations is the token of peace. By the same principle, the dove of the Holy Spirit flies to earth—to our flesh as it emerges from the bath, after its old sins [have been washed], bringing us the peace of God. This is sent out from the heavens, where lies the Church, the figurative ark. (Gal. 4:26)

However, the ancient world returned to sin, so the Deluge does not prefigure baptism in that sense. For that reason, the world is now destined to fire—the same as a man who renews his sins after baptism. So the [punishment facing the world] should be viewed as a warning for our admonition.

Examples Of Deliverance By Water

9. Notice, then, how the sanctity of water has been arranged by so many pleas of nature, privileges of grace, ceremonies of discipline, symbols, preparations, and prayers. The first, of course, was when the [Israelite] people were unconditionally set free. For they escaped the violence of the Egyptian king by crossing through *water*. And it was *water* that destroyed the king himself, with his entire forces. (Ex. 19:27-30) What symbol has been better fulfilled in the

[4]This was the general belief in Tertullian's day.

sacred mystery of baptism: peoples are set free from the world by means of water. They leave the devil—their old tyrant—quite behind, overwhelmed in the water.

Another example is Moses' restoring the water [of Marah] from "bitterness" to its native grace of "sweetness" by the [wood from a] tree. (Ex. 15:24,25) That tree prefigured Christ, restoring through himself the veins of sometime envenomed and bitter nature into the all-healthful waters of baptism. This is the water which flowed continuously down for the people from the "rock that accompanied them." (1 Cor. 10:3) Since Christ is "the Rock," we see without doubt that baptism is blessed by the water in Christ.

Christ and Water

How mighty is the grace of water in the sight of God and his Christ, for the confirmation of baptism! Never is Christ without water. First, he was himself baptized in water. Then, when he was invited to the wedding, he made the very first display of his power by using water [which he changed to wine]. Later, in his teaching, he invited the thirsty to his own everlasting water. (John 7:37,38) Again, when teaching about love, he approved the cup of water offered to a poor child. (Matt. 10:42) He replenished his strength at a well. He walked on water. He willingly crossed the sea. (Mark 4:36) And he ministered water to his disciples [i.e. washing their feet].

The witness of baptism went even to the Passion. While Jesus was being surrendered to the cross, water was present. Remember Pilate's hands [being washed with water]. And remember the soldier's lance: when Jesus was wounded, water burst out of his side. (John 29:34)

3

John's Baptism

10. Up to this point, I have spoken only of the general principles of the sanctity of baptism, to the best of my meager ability. I will now proceed to other matters concerning baptism, answering certain minor questions to the best of my ability.

The Lord himself asked the Pharisees a question about the baptism announced by John. He asked whether this baptism was heavenly or earthly. (Matt. 21:25) They were unable to give a consistent answer, for they neither understood nor believed. Yet, we, though poor in understanding and faith, are able to determine that John's baptism was indeed divine. That is, the commission was divine, for the Lord sent John to perform this duty. (John 1:33)

However, it's effectiveness was not divine, but human. For it conveyed nothing heavenly. It merely foreshadowed heavenly things. It was ordained for repentance—which is in man's power. But, in fact, the teachers of the law and the Pharisees, who were unwilling to believe, did not repent. (Matt. 3:7-12) If repentance is a human thing, baptism for repentance must be of the same nature. Otherwise, if it were heavenly, it would have given both the Holy Spirit and the remission of sins.

But only God pardons sins and freely grants the Spirit. (Mark 2:7,8; 2 Cor. 1:21, 22) Even the Lord said that the Spirit would not descend unless he would first ascend to the Father.

(John 16:6,7) What the Lord himself was not yet bestowing, the servant [John] could obviously not bestow. So in the Acts of the Apostles, we find that men who had "John's baptism" had not received the Holy Spirit. In fact, they had not even heard of the Spirit. (Acts 19:1-7) So it [John's baptism] was not a heavenly thing, for it furnished no heavenly benefits.

In fact, the very thing that was heavenly in John, the Spirit of prophecy, completely left him after the transfer of the Spirit to the Lord. For John even had to ask whether Jesus, of whom he had preached and whom he had pointed out when coming to him, was really *he*. (Matt 11:2-6; Luke 7:18-23) So "the baptism of repentance" was dealt with as if it were a candidate for the coming remission and sanctification through Christ. It's true that John preached "baptism for the remission of sins," but the declaration was referring to a *future* remission. (Mark 1:4) For repentance must precede remission, and this is "preparing the way." (Luke 1:76) The one who *prepares* does not himself complete. Rather, he obtains for someone else to complete.

John himself professed that the heavenly things were not his, but Christ's. He said, "He who is from the earth speaks concerning the earth. He who comes from the realms above is over all." (John 3:30, 31) He also said that he baptized for repentance only, but that one would shortly come who would baptize in "the Spirit and fire." (Matt.3:11) Of course, true and stable faith is baptized with *water*—for salvation. Pretended and weak faith is baptized with fire—for judgment.

Did Jesus Baptize?

11. However, some say, "But look, the Lord came; yet he did not baptize anyone. For we read, 'And yet he did not baptize, but his disciples!'" (John 4:2) As if John [the Baptist] had preached that Jesus would baptize *with his own hands*! Of course, his words do not mean that. Rather, they were said as a normal manner of speech. Similarly, we say, "The emperor set forth a decree," or, "The magistrate beat him." Pray tell, does the emperor personally set forth a decree? Does a magistrate personally beat someone? We normally

say someone has performed an act even though his stewards physically accomplish it.

So [when John said,] "He will baptize you" we must understand that to mean, "you will be baptized *through* him," or "into him." But do not be troubled by the fact that he himself did not baptize. Unto what would Jesus have baptized? Unto repentance? If that were the case, of what use was his forerunner [John]? Unto remission of sins? But he gave remission merely by a word. Unto himself? But through humility he was concealing [his true nature]. Unto the Holy Spirit? But the Spirit had not yet descended from the Father. Unto the Church? But his apostles had not yet founded the church.

In conclusion, it can be seen that his disciples, as his stewards, used to baptize with the "baptism of John." This was the same baptism with which John, as forerunner, had previously baptized. Let no one think it was with some other baptism, because none other exists, except that of Christ—which came later. At that time, of course, it [Christ's baptism] could not be given by his disciples, for the glory of the Lord had not yet been fully attained. Furthermore, the effectiveness of the bath [of baptism] had not been established through the suffering and resurrection [of Christ]. In fact, our own death cannot see an end except by the Lord's suffering, and our life cannot be restored without his resurrection.

Were The Apostles Baptized?

12. However, some have conscientious—or rather *audacious*—doubts about the rule: "Salvation is not attainable by anyone without baptism." This rule is primarily based on the Lord's statement, 'Unless one is born of water, he does not have life.' (John 3:5)

They ask, "If that rule is true, how did the apostles obtain salvation? For none of them were baptized in the Lord—except Paul. Paul was the only one of them who had put on the garment of Christ's baptism." (Gal. 3:27) They continue, "So you can maintain the rule only by placing at peril the salvation of those apostles who lacked the water of Christ. On the other hand, if you admit that salvation has been ordained even for the unbaptized, you rescind the rule."

The Lord is my witness that I have heard doubts of that kind. So please do not imagine that, with the license of my pen, I am so perverse that I have personally conjured up these ideas on my own. For these ideas would only give new misgivings to others.

To the best of my ability, I will now reply to those who say that the apostles were unbaptized. First, assuming they had undergone the human baptism of John, if they were longing for that [baptism] of the Lord, the Lord [would have answered them when] he defined baptism to be one. (Eph. 4:5) He had said to Peter, who wanted to be thoroughly bathed, "he who has once bathed has no necessity to wash a second time." (John 13:9,10) Of course, he would not have said this to one who was not baptized. Even here we have a conspicuous proof against those who, in order to destroy the sacrament of water, deny that the apostles had received even John's baptism.

Can it seem believable that "the way of the Lord," that is, the baptism of John, had not been "prepared" in those persons [the apostles] who were being destined to open the way of the Lord throughout the whole world? Even the Lord himself, who had nothing to repent of, was baptized. So baptism was surely necessary to sinners, was it not?

It is true that some persons [in Jesus' day] were not baptized. Those persons, however, were not the companions of Christ, but rather they were the enemies of the faith—the Pharisees and the teachers of the Law. From this we can make an assumption: Since those who *opposed* the Lord *refused* to be baptized, it follows that those who *followed* the Lord *were* baptized. They certainly would not have been of one mind with their own rivals.[h]

Others make the suggestion (a rather forced one) that "the apostles received baptism when, in their little ship, they were sprinkled and covered with the waves: that Peter himself also was sufficiently immersed when he walked on the sea." [Matt. 8:24; 14:28, 29] It is, however, one thing to be sprinkled or intercepted by the violence of the sea, and another thing to be baptized in obedience to the discipline of religion. But that little ship did present a figure of the Church. She is disquieted "in the sea," or in the world, "by the waves," or by persecutions and temptations. The Lord, through patience, sleeping as it were, until roused by the desperation of the prayers of the saints, he restrains the world, and restores tranquillity to his own.

Now, regardless of whether they were baptized in any manner whatever, or whether they continued unwashed to the end,[i] to determine the salvation of the apostles is still audacious. For the apostles had the distinction of being the first chosen, which was followed by undivided intimacy. These things in themselves might have been able to bestow [the equivalent of] the comprehensive grace of baptism. For the apostles followed Him who promised salvation to every believer. "Your faith," he would say, "has saved you." (Luke 18:42; Mark 10:52) And, "Your sins shall be forgiven" because of believing, even though, of course, you are not yet baptized. (Mark 2:5)

If such faith [in the Lord] was lacking in the apostles, I do not know what sort of faith it was that, roused by merely one word of the Lord, moved one apostle to leave the tax collector's booth behind forever [Matt. 9:9], another to desert his father and ship, and the trade by which he gained his living [Matt. 4:21, 22], and a third to disdain his father's funeral rites [Luke 9:59,60]. So, even before he heard it, the latter fulfilled that highest precept of the Lord, "He who prefers father or mother to me is not worthy of me." (Matt. 10:37)

4

Is Baptism Necessary For Salvation?

13. But the heretics provoke further questions. They say, "Baptism is not necessary for those to whom faith is sufficient. After all, Abraham pleased God by a sacrament of faith, not water." But in all cases it is the *later* things that have conclusive force. The later [revelation of God] prevails over the earlier. Granted, in former days there was salvation by bare faith, before the suffering and resurrection of the Lord. But now faith has been enlarged, and has become a faith that believes in his birth, suffering, and resurrection. So the ordinance [of faith] has been amplified by the addition of the sealing act of baptism. This is, so to speak, the clothing of the faith which was previously bare, which now cannot exist without its proper law.

For the law of baptizing has been imposed, and the formula prescribed: "Go," he says, "teach the nations, baptizing them into the name of the Father, and of the Son, and of the Holy Spirit."[j] (Matt. 28:19) "Unless a man has been born again of water and Spirit, he shall not enter into the kingdom of the heavens." (John 3:5) Those words have tied faith to the necessity of baptism. Accordingly, all who became believers after that time were baptized. So it was that Paul was baptized when he believed. This is the meaning of the direction which the Lord had given him when he was struck with blindness, "Arise, and enter Damascus; there it shall be demonstrated to you what you ought to do." This meant he was to be baptized, which was the only thing he lacked. For he had sufficiently learned and believed the Nazarene to be "the Lord, the Son of God." (Acts 9:1-31)

But Paul Didn't Baptize!

14. However, they throw out another objection from that apostle himself [i.e. Paul], for he said, "For Christ did not send me to baptize." (1 Cor. 1:17) As if by this argument baptism were done away with! But if that were the case, why did he baptize Gaius, and Crispus, and the house of Stephanas? (1 Cor. 1:14,16) However, even if Christ had not sent Paul to baptize, he had given other apostles the command to baptize.

The words [quoted above] were written to the Corinthians regarding the circumstances of that particular time. Schisms and dissensions were arising among them. One person attributed everything to Paul, but another to Apollos. (1 Cor. 3:3,4) For that reason, the peace-making apostle, for fear that he would seem to claim all gifts for himself, said that he had been sent "not to baptize, but to preach." For preaching precedes, while baptizing follows. So the preaching came first. But I think baptizing was certainly lawful for him [Paul] to whom preaching was lawful.

Is The Baptism Of Heretics Valid?

15. I do not know whether any further point can be debated to bring baptism into controversy. Permit me to call to mind what I have omitted above, lest I seem to break off the train of thought in the middle. There is to us one—and only one—baptism. This is according to the Lord's gospel and the apostle's letters. For he says, 'One God, one baptism, and one church' in the heavens. (Eph. 4:4-6)

Now we need to consider the question, "What rules are to be observed with regard to [baptism by] heretics?" For the reference to "one baptism" refers to *us* [i.e. the orthodox church]. Heretics, however, have no fellowship in our discipline, as the mere fact of their excommunication testifies that they are outsiders. So I am not bound to recognize in *them* a thing which is directed to *me*. For we do not have the same God, nor the same Christ, as they. Therefore, their baptism is not *one* with ours, for it is not the same. Since they do not have a proper baptism, essentially they have none at all.[k] I have already [i.e. in a previous work] discussed this point more fully in Greek.[1]

We enter the bath only once, because sins are washed away only once in that they ought never to be repeated. But the Jewish Israel bathes daily, because they are being defiled daily. For fear that defilement should be practiced among us also, the definition concerning the *one* bathing was made. (John 13:10; Eph. 4:5) This is joyful water that washes away *once*! It does not mock sinners with vain hopes. It does not, by being infected with the repetition of impurities, defile again those whom it has washed.

The Baptism Of Blood

16. However, we do have a second bath—of blood—which is actually *one* with the baptism of water. About this bath, the Lord said, "I have to be baptized with a baptism," although he had already been baptized [in water]. (Luke 12:50) For he had come "by means of water and blood," just as John has written. (1 Jn. 5:6) He was baptized by the water and glorified by the blood to make us, in the same way, called by water and chosen by blood. (Matt. 20:16; Rev. 17:14) He sent these two baptisms out from the wound in his pierced side, so that those who believed in his blood might be bathed with the water. (John 19:34) And so that those who had been bathed in the water might also drink the blood. (John 6:53) This is the baptism that stands in lieu of the water bath when that has not been received. It also restores it when it has been lost.

---

[1]It should be noted that Tertullian's view on heretical baptism was not universally shared by the early church—in particular the church at Rome. The church at Rome generally accepted water baptism performed by a heretic as being valid—on the grounds that the cleansing grace of baptism is imparted by *God*, not the person who administers the baptism.

5

The Proper Way To Baptize

17. In concluding our brief subject, I need to also review for you the proper method of giving and receiving baptism. The primary priest,[1] that is, the overseer, has the right to give it. Following him, the elders and deacons also have the right, but not without the overseer's authority because of the honor of the Church. When this honor is preserved, peace is preserved. In addition to those persons, even laymen have the right. For what is equally received can be equally given. Unless overseers, priests, or deacons be on the spot, other disciples are called to the work.

The word of the Lord should not be hidden by anyone. In the same way, baptism, which is equally God's property, can be administered by all. But how much more is the principle of reverence and modesty incumbent on laymen. They should appreciate that these powers belong to their superiors, lest they usurp for themselves the specific function of the overseer. Envy of the overseer's office is the mother of divisions. The most holy apostle has said that "all things are lawful, but not all expedient." (1 Cor. 10:23) Let it be sufficient

---

[1]The Latin term Tertullian uses here is *sacerdos*, which basically means "one who gives sacred things." During the 3rd century, elders and overseers were often referred to by the term *sacerdos*. Of course, the term was also used to refer to any Christian.

to follow that principle in cases of necessity—if the circumstances of place, time, or person makes it necessary for you [to baptize].[l] Otherwise, you will be guilty of a human creature's loss if you do not bestow what you had free liberty to bestow.[2]

Should Women Baptize?

The impudent woman, who has usurped the power to teach, will obviously not give birth to a right of baptizing, lest some new beast should arise like the former. So that just as the one abolished baptism, some other should in her own right bestow it!

However, someone may refer to a certain writing that wrongly goes under Paul's name. Through it they may claim the example of Thecla as a license for women to teach and baptize. Let them know that in Asia, the elder who composed that writing,[m] after being convicted [of writing this spurious work], and after confessing that he had done it from love of Paul, was removed from his office.[3] How believable is it that Paul, who did not permit a woman even to *learn* too brashly, would have given a female the power of teaching and baptizing! "Let them be silent," he says, "and at home consult their own husbands." (1 Cor. 14:34,35)

Don't Baptize Too Hastily!

18. But those whose duty it is, know that baptism is not to be rashly administered. The words, "Give to every one who begs you," refer primarily to charitable giving [not to baptism]. (Luke 6:30) In contrast, [in the case of baptism] a different principle should be carefully considered: "Do not give the holy thing to the dogs, nor cast your pearls before swine." (Matt. 7:6) And another, "Do not lay hands hastily on anyone; do not share other men's sins." (1 Tim. 5:22)

---

[2] i.e. you will be responsible for not baptizing someone when it was in your power to do so.

[3] Tertullian is referring here to a spurious work, generally known as the "Acts of Paul and Thecla."

It may seem that Philip hastily dipped the eunuch. But remember that the Lord had intervened in this case and had given clear and convincing evidence that he considered the eunuch worthy. For the Spirit had urged Philip to proceed to that particular road. Furthermore, the eunuch was not found idle. And he was not one who was suddenly seized with an eager desire to be dipped. Rather, after he went up to the temple for prayer and was intently absorbed in the divine Scripture, he was suitably discovered. Without being asked by the eunuch, God had sent him an apostle. This apostle had been directed by the Spirit to come up to the eunuch's chariot. The Scripture which he was reading fell in appropriately with his faith. (Acts 8:28-33; Is. 53:7, 8) Philip, being requested, sat beside him. The Lord was pointed out, and the eunuch's faith did not linger. Water was available, so the work was completed, and the apostle was snatched away.

"But," someone may say, "Paul, too, was 'quickly' baptized." Yes, but Simon, his host, quickly recognized him to be "a chosen vessel." God indicates his approval with advance notices that are certain.[n]

Baptism of Children Not Recommended

But the delay of baptism is preferable—depending on the circumstances, disposition, and even the age of each individual. This is particularly true in the case of little children. Why is it necessary (if baptism itself is not *indispensably* necessary) that the sponsors should be thrust into danger?[4] For they may fail to fulfil their promises because of their own human frailty. Or they may be disappointed by the development of an evil disposition in those [i.e. the child] for whom they stood. It's true that the Lord says, "Forbid them not to come to me." (Matt. 19:14) However, let them "come" while they're growing up. Let them "come" while they are learning—while they are learning *where* to come. Let them become Christians when they have become able to know Christ. Why

---

[4]When a young child was baptized, a sponsor assumed responsibility for the faith of the young child.

does the innocent period of life hasten to the "remission of sins?"

After all, we exercise more caution than that in mere secular matters. Is one who cannot be entrusted with earthly things to be entrusted with things that are divine? Let them first know how to "ask" for salvation. At least in that way you will have given "to him who asks."° (Matt. 5:42) If anyone appreciates the great importance of baptism, they will fear *receiving* it more than *delaying* it. For sound faith is secure of salvation.

When To Baptize

19. The Passover[5] provides a specially solemn day for baptism. For that is when the Lord's suffering, in which we are baptized, was completed. (Mark 10:38,39) And it's not inappropriate to interpret figuratively the fact that, when the Lord was about to celebrate the last Passover, he said to the disciples who were sent to make preparation, "You will meet a man bearing *water*." (Mark 14:13) So he pointed out the place for celebrating the Passover by the sign of water.

After that, the period of Pentecost[6] is a most joyous season for granting baptisms. During this period, the resurrection of the Lord was repeatedly proved to the disciples. The hope of the [second] coming of the Lord was also indirectly pointed to during this period. For when Christ had been received back into the heavens, the angels told the apostles that "he would come in the same way as he had ascended into the heavens"—at Pentecost, of course. (Acts 1:10-11) Also, Jeremiah said, "And I will gather them together from the extremities of the land in the feast-day."[7] By this he signified the day of the Passover and of Pentecost, which is properly a "feast-day."

---

[5]What is generally today called "Good Friday" in English speaking countries, was called "Passover" by the early Christians.

[6]Tertullian is referring to the entire 50 day period between Passover (Easter) and Pentecost.

[7]Tertullian is following the reading of the Septuagint, which reads differently in this passage than most English translations.

However, *every* day is the Lord's. So every hour, every time, is appropriate for baptism. If there is a difference in the solemnity, there is none in the grace.

Preparation For Baptism

20. Those who are about to be baptized should pray with repeated prayers, fasts, bendings of the knee, and all-night vigils. They should confess all past sins, so that they can express the meaning even of the baptism of John: "They were baptized," it says "confessing their own sins." (Matt. 3:6) To us it is a matter for thankfulness if we now publicly confess our sins or base deeds.[8] By doing so, we make satisfaction for our former sins, through the mortification of the flesh and spirit. And we lay the foundation for a defense against the temptations that will closely follow.

"Watch and pray," he says "lest you fall into temptation." (Matt. 26:41) And the reason, I believe, they [the apostles] were tempted was that they fell asleep. As a result, they deserted the Lord when he was arrested. The one [Peter] who continued to stand by him, and used the sword, even denied him three times. The word had gone before, that 'no one untempted should attain the heavenly kingdoms.' (Matt. 10:38,39) After his baptism, the Lord himself was surrounded by temptations when he had fasted for forty days.

Someone may say, "Then we too should fast after baptism." Well, who forbids you? Unless it be the necessity for joy, and the thanksgiving for salvation. But so far as I understand, with my poor powers, the Lord [by his fasting] figuratively brought back upon Israel the reproach they had cast on the Lord.

For the people had crossed the sea and had wandered about in the desert for forty years. Even though they were nourished there with divine provisions, they were more mindful of their belly and gullet than of God. In contrast, the Lord, driven into desert places after baptism, maintained a

---

[8]If we confess our sins now, they are forgiven. It is too late to confess them on judgment day.

fast of forty days. He thereby showed that the man of God lives 'not by bread alone, but by the word of God.' (Matt. 4:1-4) He also showed that temptations that come from an immoderate appetite are shattered by abstinence.

Therefore, blessed ones, whom the grace of God awaits, when you ascend from that most sacred bath of your new birth, spread your hands [in prayer] for the first time in the house of your mother.[9] And, together with your brothers, ask from the Father, ask from the Lord, that his own specialties of grace and distributions of gifts be supplied to you. (1 Cor. 12:4-12) "Ask," he says, "and you shall receive." (Matt. 7:7) Well, you *have* asked, and you have received. You *have* knocked, and it has been opened to you. Only, I pray that, when you are asking, you remember Tertullian the sinner in your petition.

---

[9]Early Christians often referred to the Church as their mother, based on Gal. 4:26.

On The Veiling Of Virgins

Introduction

The final work in this volume requires a brief introduction. Outside of the conservative Brethren, Amish, and Mennonite groups and the Catholic and Orthodox nuns, the modern Western churches have almost universally ignored the apostolic teaching on the prayer veil found in 1 Corinthians 11:2-16.

However, discarding the prayer veil is actually a fairly recent development in the church. From the first century to well into the nineteenth century, Christian women of virtually every denomination wore the prayer covering. Browse through some illustrated history books and notice the pictures of Christian women through the centuries. You will find that almost invariably they were wearing some sort of head covering. The caps worn by the Pilgrims [i.e. Separatists] and the Puritans were not there for decoration. They were a prayer covering. And so were the scarfs worn by women in Eastern Europe.

In the early church, the issue was not whether or not a woman should wear a head covering, but what did Paul mean by the term "woman?" The Greek word *gyne* can mean "woman," "married woman," or "wife." So when Paul wrote to the Corinthians that every *gyne* should pray with her head veiled, it's not clear in itself whether he was including virgins in his instructions. So some churches required that all mature females be covered, but others required only married women to be covered. It was this difference in practice that led Tertullian to write his tract, in which he argued that all mature females should be veiled.

As so many lawyers are inclined to do, Tertullian ends up over-proving his case. His best argument is his appeal for his reader to look at the practice of the Christians in Corinth. After all, it was to them that Paul addressed his letter. How did they understand his instructions? Another good argument is his plea for his reader to observe the other churches where one or more of the apostles had personally taught, such as Rome, Ephesus, and Antioch. However, Tertullian proceeds to throw out every other argument imaginable, including Montanistic revelations and angelic visits. In the end, he weakens his argument by over-proving his case.

Nevertheless, this tract gives the modern church priceless insight into the apostolic command that a woman should not pray or prophesy with her head uncovered. It reveals how the Christians closest to the apostles understood his commandment. It also destroys so many modern myths about veiling. For example, one of the common assertions made today is that Paul wanted the Corinthian women to be veiled merely so that they wouldn't be mistaken for prostitutes. I'm not sure who invented that story. But whoever did fabricated it out of thin air. There is nothing in any of the early Christian writings to support such a view. In fact, as Tertullian's tract demonstrates, the issue wasn't the wearing of a veil out in the streets, for all Christian women were doing that anyway. The issue was wearing the veil among the brethren.

Montanism

In addition to giving us insight on the prayer veil, this tract also gives us much insight into Montanism. Tertullian wrote this work after he joined the Montanist, or New Prophecy, movement. Although this sect was orthodox in theology, it differed from the main body of the church in claiming that the Holy Spirit was still giving new special revelation to Christians. In contrast, the main body of the church taught that special revelation ended with the apostles.

The Montanists were a rigorous, ascetic sect with many obligatory fasts and disciplinary rules not followed by the Church. They taught that it was wrong to flee from persecution, and they did not allow second marriages for any reason, even the death of one's spouse. Although the Church encouraged celibacy, the Montanists went much further, often treating marriage as something impure.

One of the distinguishing features of Montanism was its heavy emphasis on prophecy, visions and angelic visits. It was primarily the women in this movement who experienced these things. You will find several references to such revelations in the tract that follows. Whether or not these supernatural revelations were really from God, I will let the reader decide.

1

Truth Or Custom?

1. Having already undergone the trouble distinctive of my opinion, I will demonstrate in Latin[1] that it is necessary that our virgins be veiled from the time that they reach adolescence. This observation is demonstrated by *truth* itself. Therefore, nobody can place any restriction on this practice—whether because of lapse of time, influence of persons, or geographical privileges. For such things are, for the most part, the reasons why *customs* originate.[a] And customs eventually become the norm and thereby stand in opposition to truth. For our Lord Christ referred to himself as "the Truth"—not, "the Custom." Since Christ is everlasting and is prior to all, truth is therefore ancient and everlasting.

So if that which is actually old seems *new* to you, the problem lies with yourself. It is not something new that points out heresies. Rather, truth does. So whatever stands in opposition to truth is heresy—even though it may be an ancient custom.[b]

The rule of faith, indeed, is entirely *one*—immovable and unchangeable. That rule is this: to believe in only one almighty God, the Creator of the universe; and in his Son Jesus Christ, born of the virgin Mary, crucified under Pontius Pilate, raised again from the dead on the third day, received

[1]Tertullian had apparently written a previous tract on this subject in Greek. However, there are no extant copies of that work.

in the heavens, sitting now at the right hand of the Father, destined to come to judge the living and the dead through the resurrection of the flesh as well as of the spirit.[2]

The Montanist View Of Progressive Prophecy

Although the law of faith is constant, the matters of discipline and conversation that follow it are susceptible to new corrections. For the grace of God continues to operate, and it progresses up to the end [of the world]. After all, what kind of logic is it that acknowledges that the devil is always operating and adding new forms of wickedness every day, but that the work of God has ceased—or at least, that it has made no new advancements? In fact, the very reason why the Lord sent the Paraclete [i.e. the Holy Spirit] was that human weakness was unable to take in all things at once. Therefore, discipline had to be directed, ordained, and brought to perfection little by little by the Holy Spirit, the Vicar of the Lord.

He said, "Still, I have many things to say to you, but you are not yet able to bear them. When that Spirit of truth shall have come, he will conduct you into all truth, and will report to you the things to come.[c] (John 16:12,13) What, then, is the Paraclete's administrative office, other than this: to direct discipline to reveal the Scriptures, to form the intellect anew, and to advance toward "the better things." (Heb. 11:40)

Nothing is without stages of growth. All things await their season. In short, the preacher said, "There is a time for everything." (Ecc. 3:1) Look how creation itself advances little by little to fruition. First comes the seed. From the seed arises the shoot. Next, the shrub struggles forth from the shoot. Then branches and leaves grow strong. This plant, which we now call a tree, continues to grow larger. Finally, buds appear. From the buds burst forth blossoms. And fruit comes out from the blossom. At first the fruit is unfinished and unshapely. But little by little, following the straight

---

[2]This is an early form of the well known "Apostles Creed."

course of its development, it is trained to the ripeness of its flavor.

Now, the God of righteousness and of creation is the same. So, righteousness was likewise originally in an incomplete state, having only a natural fear of God. But from that stage it advanced to infancy through the Law and the Prophets. From there, through the Gospel, it advanced to the vigor of youth. Now, through the Paraclete, it is coming into maturity. After Christ, He is the only one to be called and revered as Master. (Matt. 23:8) For he speaks not of himself, but that which is commanded by Christ. (John 16:13) He is the only Prelate, because he alone succeeds Christ. Those who have received him set truth before custom. Those who have heard him prophesying up to the present time (not of old) command virgins to be wholly covered.[3]

The General Practice Of The Church On Veiling

2. Nevertheless, for the sake of argument, I will, for the moment, not attribute this rule [of veiling virgins] to truth. Rather, I will attribute it to custom. In this way, I can oppose one custom with that of another. For throughout Greece, and certain of its barbaric provinces, the majority of churches keep their virgins covered. In fact, this practice is followed in certain places beneath this African sky. So let no one ascribe this custom merely to the Gentile customs of the Greeks and barbarians.

Moreover, I will put forth as models those churches that were founded by either apostles or apostolic men.[d] These churches, as well as others, have the self-same authority of custom to appeal to. For they have in their arsenal both antiquity and a line of respected teachers—more so than those churches founded later.[4] So whom do we follow? Which practice are we to choose?

---

[3]"Those who have heard him prophesying up to the present time" refers to the Montanists.

[4]Among most early Christians, the doctrines and practices of those churches where the apostles had personally taught were considered a general standard for orthodoxy

We can't hastily dismiss a custom that we are unable to condemn. And we can't condemn such a custom, for it is not "strange." By that, I mean it is not found among "strangers," but rather among those churches with whom we share the law of peace and the name of brotherhood. Both they and we have the same "one faith," "one God," the same Christ, the same hope, and the same baptismal mysteries.[5] Let me say it once for all, we are *one Church*. So whatever belongs to our brothers is ours. Only, the body divides us.

This issue should be handled by the same method we handle all other issues where there are a variety of practices. Or where there is doubt and uncertainty. That method is to make examination to see which of the two different customs is the more compatible with the discipline of God. [If we use this method in the present instance], we, of course, will choose the custom that keeps virgins veiled. Such virgins are known to God alone. For their glory must be sought from God, not from men. And such virgins ought to blush even at their own privilege.

For you cause a virgin to blush more by praising her than by blaming her.[e] For your custom deceives virgins while it exhibits them [unveiled]. Such a custom would never have been approved by anybody except those men who must have been similar in character to the virgins themselves. Such eyes want a virgin to be seen. Similarly, the eyes of such virgins wish to be seen. So the same kind of eyes mutually crave after each other. For *seeing* and *being seen* belong to the self-same lust. To blush if he should see a virgin is the mark of a holy man—just as much as it is the mark of a holy virgin to blush if seen by a man.

3. In fact, those most "sanctified" teachers have not even bothered to examine between customs. Still, until very recently, among us either custom was admitted to communion with comparative indifference. The matter had been left up to each virgin to choose either to veil herself or to

---

[5]The Latin word here is *sacramenti*, which is the Latin equivalent of the Greek word *mysteria*

expose herself. Just as she had equal liberty in choosing to marry, which is neither required nor prohibited.

In effect, Truth was content to compromise with Custom, so that, under the name of Custom, Truth would at least be followed by some. But when the power of discerning began to advance,[f] immediately the great Adversary of good things—and much more of good practices—went to work. In opposition to the virgins of God, the virgins of men go about with front quite bare, spurred on to a rash audacity.[g]

Is Veiling A Scandal?

"We are scandalized," such virgins say, "because others follow a different practice than we do."[6] So they prefer to feel "scandalized" than to practice modesty. But, if I am not mistaken, a scandal is an example of something bad, not good. It is something that leads to sinful edification. Good things scandalize no one but those with an evil mind. And modesty, quietness, contempt of glory, and desire to please only God—these are good things. Let those women who are "scandalized" by such good things learn to admit their own evil.

What if married persons said they were "scandalized" by those who remain celibate? Would we forbid celibacy? Should monogamy be thrown out for fear the polygamists might be "scandalized?" Rather, shouldn't it be the chaste virgins who deserve to complain that the immodesty and brashness of showy virginity is a "scandal" to them?

For the sake of these marketable creatures [i.e. the unveiled virgins], are the chaste virgins to be dragged into the church—blushing at being recognized in public, quaking at being unveiled—as though they had been invited, so to speak, to be raped? For, they are no more willing to be unveiled than they would to be violated. To an honorable virgin, every public exposure is the equivalent of being raped. In fact, the suffering of carnal violence is less evil

[6]The virgins who did not veil themselves were apparently complaining that the veiled virgins were "scandalizing" them.

because it is not of her own volition. But when the very spirit itself is violated in a virgin by the removal of her covering, she has become accustomed to losing what she used to keep.

Oh sacrilegious hands! Hands that have the audacity to rip off a dress dedicated to God! What worse could any persecutor have done? Particularly if he had known that this garment had been chosen by a virgin? You have stripped bare the head of a virgin. And thereafter she wholly ceases to be a virgin to herself. She has undergone a change!

Arise, therefore, Truth! Arise, and burst forth from your patient waiting. I do not wish you to defend *any* custom. For, in these times, even that custom under which you enjoyed your own liberty is now being stormed.[7] Demonstrate that it is you yourself who are the one who covers virgins. Interpret in person your own Scriptures, which Custom does not understand. For if Custom had, she never would have come into existence.

---

[7] Apparently, the custom of allowing virgins to choose either to veil, or not to veil, was being criticized in some churches, and in those churches all virgins were being instructed *not* to wear the veil.

2

Is A Virgin A "Woman"?

4. Nevertheless, it is customary for persons to try to argue from the Scriptures in opposition to truth. So some argue against us, "The apostle made no mention of *virgins* when he laid down the rule about the veil, for he only mentions *women*.[1] If he had meant for virgins to be covered as well, he would have specifically mentioned both virgins and women. For in his passage about marriage he gave specific counsel to virgins." (1 Cor. 7:1-40) So those who oppose us conclude, "Virgins are not included in the law of veiling the head, since they are not named in this law. In fact, this is the reason that our virgins are not veiled. Since they are not specifically named, they are not commanded."

But I will use the same argument in reply: He [Paul] knew how to specifically address both kinds of females—virgin and woman (non-virgin)—when he *wanted* to make a distinction. (1 Cor. 7:1-40) So in those passages where he does not make specific mention of virgins, it means he did not wish to make a distinction. He is indicating that their conditions are identical. Otherwise, in this passage [1 Cor. 11], he could have pointed out the difference between [what was required] of a virgin and a woman. For elsewhere he said, "There is a

[1]The Greek word *gyne,* and its Latin equivalent *mulier,* can mean "woman," "married woman," or "wife." So when Paul wrote to the Corinthians that every *gyne* should pray with her head veiled, it's not clear in itself whether he was including virgins in his instructions.

difference between a woman and a virgin." (1 Cor. 7:34) So when he is silent about virgins, he has made no distinction. Rather, he has included virgins in the term "women."

But the aforementioned "difference between a woman and a virgin" does not apply to the present issue, although some would argue that it does. There are many sayings [in Scripture] that address a particular situation, and they have no application to matters not under discussion. One saying can apply to two situations only when the subject matter is the same. The discussion where woman and virgin are distinguished [1 Cor. 7:1- 40] is not connected to the present question.

He [Paul] says, "The woman and the virgin are divided." Why? Because "the unmarried," that is, the virgin, "is anxious about those things which are the Lord's, that she may be holy both in body and in spirit. But the married," that is, the non-virgin, "is anxious how she may please her husband." (1 Cor. 7:34) That is what is meant by the two being "divided." So that principle has no application to the subject at hand. For our subject is not about marriage, nor about the mind and thoughts of women and virgins. It is about the veiling of the head.

And concerning this veiling, the Holy Spirit makes no distinction [between a woman and a virgin]. The Spirit in tended that the one designation "woman" would include the virgin as well. By not making any special reference to virgins, He has included the virgin with the "woman." Is it really something new to use a general term [such as "woman"] and yet to include within the term any special class [such as "virgin"]? Particularly where there is no need to distinguish all of the different members of the class?[h]

Let's proceed, then, to the word in question. The natural word that expresses the distinction [of gender] is "female." Under this term is the general word "woman." Again, under the general word are the special terms, "virgin," "wife," "widow," and other such designations (including those that distinguish between age groups). The special term is included in the general term.[i]

Accordingly, when you say "body," you do not need to make special mention of the hand, foot, or any other of its parts. Or when you say "the universe," you are including both heaven and the things in it—such as the sun, moon, stars, and constellations. You will also be including the earth, the seas, and everything that comprises the elements of the earth. By using the general term, you have included all of the parts that make up the whole. So, too, by using the term "woman," he [Paul] has included whatever is of womankind.

The First "Woman" Was A Virgin

5. Nevertheless, since those who disagree with us use the term "woman" to refer only to a female who has known a man, we must further demonstrate that this term applies to the female sex, and not to a particular type of female. For virgins as well as other females are included in this term.

First, it should be noted that when God created the second type of human being, female, to assist man, she was immediately named "woman." She was still joyful, still worthy of paradise, and still *virgin.* Adam said, "She will be called "woman." (Gen. 2:23) So the term "woman" not only includes a virgin, but in fact is *appropriate* to a virgin. In fact, this designation was first applied to a virgin.

However, some try to ingeniously argue that Adam was speaking of the future, for he said, "She *will* be called woman." That is, she would be called "woman" once she had given up her virginity. For immediately after those words, he said, "For this reason, a man shall leave father and mother, and be joined to his own woman; and the two shall be one flesh."[2] (Gen. 2:24)

In reply we say, "Let those who make this argument [that the name 'woman' was a future designation] tell us what name she had in the meantime." For without a name expressive of her present quality, she could not have been.[j] For

[2]Although many modern translations attribute these words to the narrator of Genesis, Tertullian (and perhaps most other early Christians) understood these words to have been spoken by Adam.

Adam gave names to all the animals. And he chose those names on the basis of the *present* purpose to which they were suited—not on the basis of some future condition.[k] So what was she originally called? Why, as often as she is named in the Scripture, she is designated as "woman." And this was before she was ever married. Even when she was a virgin, she was never called "virgin."

The name "woman" was the only name she initially had. And at that time nothing had yet been spoken prophetically about her. For the Scripture states that "the two were naked, Adam and his *woman*." (Gen. 2:25) And this was not said in prediction of her becoming his "wife." For his woman was at that time unmarried, being formed from his own substance. For he said, "This bone out of my bones, and flesh out of my flesh, will be called woman."

Our custom of calling our wives our "women" became the ordinary usage of common speech, without men thinking about it.[l] From the tacit consciousness of nature, the actual divinity of the soul brought about this manner of speaking. We follow this custom regardless of how incorrectly we thereby may be speaking. Now, the Greeks use the term "woman" in the sense of "wife" more often than we do. But they too have other names appropriate to "wife."

But I think this manner of speaking is actually a testimony to Scripture. For two are made into one flesh through the marriage bond. And she who is the 'flesh of flesh and bone of bones' is called the "woman" of the husband. For by being made his wife, she begins to be considered 'one flesh' with his substance. So, by nature, "woman" is not a substitute name for "wife." Rather, by condition, "wife" is a name of "woman." Wifehood cannot exist apart from womanhood, but womanhood can exist apart from wifehood.[m]

[Now let me address the words,] "On this account shall a man leave father and mother." (Gen. 2:24) The name [woman] has no connection to this prophecy, just as the prophecy has no connection to the first woman. Adam surely did not utter the prophecy with reference to Eve. Instead, he was speaking of *future* females who would be included in the maternal fountain of the feminine race. Since Adam had no [earthly] father and mother, he certainly did not leave father and mother for the sake of Eve. Since those words did not apply to Adam, they could not apply to Eve either. The words are a prophecy of how it would be with [future] husbands, who were destined to leave their parents for a woman's sake. This situation applied to neither Adam nor Eve.

Seeing this to be the case, it is readily apparent that Eve was not named "woman" because of some future circumstance. The reason is that the supposed circumstance [i.e. the prophecy of Gen. 2:24] did not apply to her. Actually, it should be noted that Adam himself stated the reason why he chose the name ["woman"]. After saying the words, "She will be called woman," he then said, "for she has been taken out of man." You should note that the man himself was still a virgin. (But I will speak, too, about the name of "man" in its own place.) Therefore, let no one interpret the name "woman" as being chosen in reference to that prophecy. For we know that it was chosen for another reason.

This is even more true when we recognize that she was given an additional name [Eve] that *was* based upon a future circumstance. (But the natural name [woman] had preceded the personal name [Eve]). Since the name "Eve" means "the mother of the living," she was so named with reference to a future circumstance. Look! It is now foretold that she is to be a wife, and not a virgin. "Eve" will be the name of one who is about to marry. For a mother comes from a bride.[n] I think I have now answered this question sufficiently.

The Virgin Mary Was A "Woman"

6. Now let us see whether or not the apostle [Paul] follows this *normal* use of the term "woman." That is, does he use it to refer to the [female] sex, the same way Genesis does?

First, [I should ask], "Does he refer to the virgin Mary as a 'woman,' just like Genesis refers to Eve?" In answer, notice what he wrote to the Galatians, saying, "God sent his own Son, made of a woman." (Gal. 4:4) Yet, you recognize that Mary was a virgin, although Hebion[2] rejects this teaching. I,

[2]Tertullian supposes Hebion to be the founder of a sect called the Ebionites, who viewed Jesus as simply an earthly Messiah, denying his virgin birth.

too, recognize that the angel Gabriel was sent to a virgin. But when he blessed her, he classified her among "women," not among "virgins." He said, "Blessed are you among *women*." (Luke 1:26, 27) So the angel knew that a virgin is [properly] called a "woman."

However, someone has apparently cleverly argued, "Both the angel and the apostle refer to Mary as a 'woman' only because she was engaged to be married. For *in some sense*, an engaged girl is a bride." However, there is a considerable difference between truth and "some sense." This is particularly true in the matter at hand.[o] For they [Gabriel and Paul] refer to Mary as a "woman," not because they considered her already married, but because she was a female. They would still have called her a woman even if she had not been engaged.[p] If Mary is called a "woman," not because of being female, but because of being assigned to a husband, then Christ was not born of a virgin. For according to this argument, one who is engaged has ceased to be a "virgin." However, since He *was* born of a virgin—who was still untouched even though she was engaged—you must admit that even an untouched virgin is called a "woman."[q]

3

The Reasons For Veiling

7. Now let's turn to the *reasons* why the apostle taught that a female should be veiled. Then we can see if the same reasons apply to virgins as well [as married women]. If the same reasons for the veil apply equally to both virgins and non-virgins, then this will further demonstrate that the same term [woman] applies to both.

Headship Of The Man

As "the man is head of the woman," he is of course head of the virgin too.[1] For the married woman was once a virgin. (Unless someone wants to argue that a virgin is a third classification of humans. And this would make her some unnatural thing with a head of its own.) As "it is shameful for a *woman* to be shaven or shorn," it is of course the same with a virgin. (If the world, God's rival, wants to assert that close-cut hair is graceful to a virgin and that flowing hair is becoming to a boy, let them demonstrate it.) So to her to whom it is unbecoming to be shaven or shorn, it is equally becoming to be covered. If "woman is the glory of man," how much more so is the virgin, who is also a glory to herself. For,

[1]Unless indicated otherwise, all of the Scriptural quotations in this chapter are from 1 Corinthians 11:3-16.

since "woman is of the man" and is "for the sake of man," it should be noted that she who was formed from the rib of Adam was first a virgin.

"Because Of The Angels"

If "the woman ought to have power upon her head," even more so should the virgin. For it is particularly *virgins* who have need for such 'power upon the head.' For "on account of the angels" refers to those angels that fell from God and heaven because of lust for females.[2] And surely those angels did not lust after females whose bodies were already defiled. They did not lust after those women who were relics of someone else's human lust. Instead, isn't it more likely that they were inflamed for *virgins*, whose bloom also is used as an excuse for human lust?

The Scripture itself suggests this understanding, for it says, "And it came to pass when men had begun to grow more numerous upon the earth, there were daughters born to them. But the sons of God, having noticed the daughters of men, that they were beautiful, took for themselves all of the wives whom they chose." (Gen. 6:1,2) Now, here the Greek term "women"[3] does seem to have the sense of "wives," since mention is made of marriage. So, in contrast, the expression, "daughters of men," obviously refers to virgins. For virgins would still be considered as belonging to their parents. But married women are called their husbands'. Notice, too, that the passage doesn't refer to these females as the 'wives of men.'

Furthermore, it doesn't call the angels *adulterers*, but husbands. And it says they took unmarried "daughters of men," who were born to men. Again, this indicates their virginity. They were first *born* and then married to angels. We know nothing else about them except they were born and were subsequently married. So perilous a face, then, that has cast

---

[2]Not all of the early Christians shared Tertullian's view that the phrase, "because of the angels," refers to the fallen angels spoken of in Genesis and in the Book of Enoch.

[3]Tertullian is quoting from the Septuagint, which uses the Greek word *gyne* here.

stumbling blocks as far as heaven ought to be shaded. In this way, when standing in the presence of God, at whose bench it stands accused of the driving of the angels from their native abode, it may blush before the other angels as well. And it can repress that former evil liberty of its head—a liberty that now is not even to be exhibited before human eyes.

But even if those angels had desired women already contaminated, so much more would it have been the duty of virgins to be veiled "on account of the angels." For it would have been the more possible for virgins to have been the reason for the angels' sinning.

The Witness Of Nature

The apostle further adds the prejudgment of "nature," saying that the abundance of hair is an honor to a woman, because hair serves for a covering. Again, this is particularly a distinction of virgins. For their very adornment properly consists in this: their hair wholly covers the very citadel of their heads with an encirclement of hair because it is massed together upon the crown.

The Relationship Of Man And Woman

8. The other side of all of these considerations is that a *man* is *not* to cover his head. He has not been gifted by nature with an excess of hair. To be shaven or shorn is not shameful to him. For it was not on *his* account that the angels transgressed. And finally, his head is Christ.

So the apostle was discussing the relationships of *man* and *woman:* why the woman should be veiled; why the man should not. That is why he was silent as to virgins. For he included virgins in the term "woman," the same way he included young males in the term "man." So he has embraced all members of each sex in the terms "man" and "woman." Similarly, while still a virgin, Adam was designated in Genesis by the name "man." For it says, 'She will be called woman, because she has been taken from her own *man.*' So Adam was a "man" before marital relations—the same as Eve was a "woman."

So, on both sides of the matter, the apostle has written with sufficient clarity to the universal species of both sexes. In fact, he says quite succinctly and plainly, "*every* woman." What does "every" mean if it doesn't mean every class, every order, every condition, every dignity, and every age? "Every" means total and entire, excluding none of its parts. And the virgin is a part of womankind.

In the same manner, when speaking of not veiling the man, he also uses the term "every." Look! Two diverse names, Man and Woman. In both cases, he includes everyone: two laws, mutually distinctive. On the one hand, a law of veiling. On the other hand, a law of not veiling.[r] If a *virgin* is not a *woman*, neither is a *young male* a *man*. If a virgin is not covered on the grounds that she is not a woman, then an adolescent male should be covered on the grounds that he is not a man. Let there be equality of privilege between male and female virgins. If female virgins are not required to be veiled, then young males should not be forbidden to be veiled.

We treat the apostle's terminology as being absolute with regards to "every *man*." We don't give discourses over the fact that he doesn't specify *young males* also. So why do we straddle the truth when it comes to "every *woman*?"

"If Anyone Is Contentious..."

Finally, he says, "If anyone is contentious, we have no such custom, nor has the church of God." He thereby shows that there had been some contention about this point. To eliminate any contention, he uses language that is all-inclusive: On the one hand, he does not specifically name the virgin, to show that there is to be no doubt about her veiling. On the other hand, he names "every *woman*." If the issue had been limited to virgins, he would have said "every *virgin*." The Corinthians themselves understood him to speak in this manner. For to this very day the Corinthians veil their virgins. What the apostles taught, the disciples of the apostles confirmed.

Virgins Are Under The Same Commandments As Married Women

9. In summation, I have discussed the argument from nature. And I have shown that veiling applies to virgins as well as to other females. Let us now look at the question of whether or not the rules of church discipline concerning women apply equally to virgins.

It is not permitted for a woman to speak in the church. (1 Cor. 14:34,35; 1 Tim. 2:11,12) And neither is it permitted for her to teach. Nor is she permitted to baptize, to offer [communion], or to claim to herself a lot in any masculine function—let alone, to assume any priestly office. Now, are any of these things lawful to a virgin? They are not. Rather, a virgin is subject to the same rules as a "woman." The need for humility is assigned to her along with the "woman." So on what grounds should this one thing [not veiling] be lawful to her when it is not lawful for any other female?

Because someone is a virgin, and has proposed to sanctify her flesh,[4] why should that give her special privileges over other women? Is the reason she is allowed to dispense with the veil so that she will stand out and be noticed when she enters the church? Is it so she may display the honor of sanctity through the liberty of her head? If so, it would have certainly been a more worthy distinction to have conferred upon her some prerogative of masculine rank or office.

I know for a fact that in a certain place a virgin who is less than twenty years old has been placed in the order of *widows*! (1 Tim. 5:9,10) Now, if the overseer needed to give her material aid, he could have done it in some other way than to set aside regulations. A virgin *widow*? Such a miracle, not to say imaginary creature, should not be pointed at in the church. The situation is even more preposterous in that even as a "widow" she does not veil her head. She denies herself

[4]Many Christian maidens made a commitment or pledge to remain virgins the rest of their lives, and they lived together with other virgins. (1 Tim. 5:11,12)

either way. She denies her virginity by being counted as a widow. She denies her widowhood by being called a virgin.

But the authority that permits her to sit in that seat [of widows] uncovered is the same which allows her to sit there in the first place as a virgin.[5] For the qualifications to be appointed to sit in that seat are as follows: Being sixty years old. Not only being the wife of one husband (which means she cannot be unmarried), but also being a *mother* and the educator of children. (1 Tim. 5:9) These [regulations] were given so that the widows would be trained through experience in all types of situations. As a result, they will be capable of readily helping all others with counsel and comfort. In addition, the regulations ensure that they will have been tested in all situations where a female might be tested. But there is no such public honor permitted to a *virgin* on the grounds of *her* position.

Male Virgins Are Not Given Special Privileges

10. Furthermore, such is not permitted for the purpose of any distinction whatsoever. And it would be rather rude [to virgin men] for females (subject as they are in all areas to men) to bear some mark of honor for *their* virginity [i.e. not being veiled]. Such a mark would cause them to be looked up to and gazed upon from all directions by their brethren. Yet, there are so many virgin men—so many voluntary eunuchs—who must carry their glory in secret. They carry no visible sign that would make them, too, illustrious.

Furthermore, celibate men will probably want to claim some distinguishing mark for themselves: Perhaps [to wear] the feathers of the Garamantes. Or else the laces of the barbarians. Maybe the cicadas of the Athenians. Or perhaps the curls of the Germans, or else the tattoos of the Britons. Or perhaps they will take the opposite course of the female virgins and will lurk in the churches with veiled heads. For surely the Holy Spirit would have made some concession to males if he had done so for females.

---

[5] i.e., there is no authority for either practice.

After all, in addition to the authority of their sex, it would have been more appropriate for males to have been honored for *their* celibacy. I say this because the male attraction to females is so strong. And because of this strong attraction, male virgins must maintain even more self-control [than female virgins]. Therefore, their celibacy is worthier of outward show, if outward show of virginity can be called "dignity."

But isn't sexual abstinence superior to virginity? And this is so whether it is the abstinence of one who is widowed, or of those who by consent have already renounced the common disgrace that matrimony involves.[6] For continual virginity is maintained by grace. But continual abstinence is maintained by virtue. For the struggle is great to overcome sexual desire once a person is accustomed to such desire. It is much easier to control such desire when a person has never known the enjoyment of it. For he does not grapple with the enemy of sexual experience.

That being the case, why, then, would God have failed to make any such concession to men, more so than to women. For this would perhaps be expected on the ground of the man's nearer intimacy [with God], being made in His "own image." Or perhaps on the grounds of the harder toil required [for a male virgin]. So if no such concessions have been made for the male, how much more so have they not been made for the female.

---

[6]The Montanists seem to have held a fairly low view of marriage. The two leading prophetesses of the movement, Maximilla and Priscilla, had both left their husbands to help lead this movement.

4

At What Age Should Veiling Begin?

11. I now need to address a matter I intentionally omitted in the preceding discussion so as to not break my continuity. I stated that the apostle's expression, "every woman," meant females of *every* age. Someone may reply by way of counter-argument that this would mean that a virgin would have to be veiled from the moment of her birth—as soon as she was enrolled as a member of the human race.

But that is not the case. She [needs to be veiled] only from the time when she begins to be conscious of, and awakens to her feminine nature. That is, when she awakens to the sense of being a female. And when she emerges from the sensation of a young girl, and she experiences that new sensation that belongs to the next stage [of maturity]. For Adam and Eve, the founders of the [human] race, went naked as long as they were without perception. But after they tasted of the tree of knowledge, the first thing they were conscious of was their cause for shame. So they marked their awareness of their sexual differences by a covering.

Since it is 'on account of the angels' that she is to be veiled, the rule of veiling will come into effect when a girl[1] reaches

---

[1]The Latin term *virgo* can mean "girl," "virgin," or "young woman." For each place that Tertullian uses *virgo* , I have tried to select the English term that best fits his meaning in that particular sentence.

the age at which the 'daughters of men' were able to invite sexual passion and to enter into marriage. For a girl ceases to be a girl when she reaches the age that it becomes possible for her *not* to be a virgin. Accordingly, among the people of Israel, it is unlawful to deliver a girl to a husband before the witness by blood of her maturity. (Deut. 22:13-21) So prior to this indication, she is not yet of age. Accordingly, if she is considered a girl as long as she is not of age, she ceases to be a girl when she becomes of age. Now, as no longer a girl, she becomes subject to the law, just as she is subject to marriage.

The Example Of Rebecca

A virgin who is engaged to be married has Rebecca as an example. When Rebecca, who was still unknown, was being taken to her husband-to-be, whom she had never met, she sighted a man in the distance and learned that he was her future husband. She immediately confessed what she had felt—namely that she was already married in spirit. She did not wait to first grasp his hand. Or to meet with a kiss. Or to exchange greetings. So she denied herself the status of virgin by immediately veiling herself. (Gen. 24:64,65) Here was a woman who already belonged to Christ's discipline! For she demonstrated that marriage can be transacted by the mind and by one's gaze—the same as fornication can. (Matt. 5:28)

Now, some do still veil a "Rebecca" [i.e. a virgin who is betrothed]. However, with regard to the rest—that is, those who are not engaged—let the procrastination of their parents, arising from rigid means or strict scruples, look to them. Let the vow of virginity look to them.

However, such procrastination can in no way pertain to that age that is already running its own assigned course and paying its own dues to maturity. For now another secret mother, Nature, and another secret father, Time, have married their daughter to their own laws. Look! Your virgin daughter is already married. Her soul is married by expectancy and her flesh by transformation. So, in effect, you are preparing her for a "second" husband. For already her voice has changed. Her limbs are fully formed. She is everywhere clothing herself to cover her shame. And the months are paying their dues. Are you going to deny that she is a woman when you know she is undergoing womanly experiences?

If someone is going to argue that it is the contact of a man that makes a female a *woman*, then let there be no covering except after the marriage union actually takes place. Yet, even among the pagans, a bride is led veiled to her husband. She is veiled at the betrothal. For then she has mingled in body and spirit with a man. That is, through the kiss and [holding] the right hands. It is through these means that they first unveiled their modesty in spirit.[s]

But even the pagans observe the rule of Time. In obedience to the law of nature, they render to each of the age groups their own rights. They send out their females to their businesses from the age of twelve years. And they send the males out two years later. They thereby decree puberty to be a function of *age*, not of engagement or marriage. Although she is still a virgin, a young maiden is called a housemother. And a young man is called a housefather, although he is only a teenager. However, *we* don't even observe natural laws. We must think the God of nature is some other God than ours!

12. A woman—in fact, a married woman—should be recognized by the testimony of both her body and her spirit. She experiences these in both conscience and in flesh. For these are the earlier records of *natural* weddings and engagements. And an external veil should be required of her who already has an internal covering. She whose lower body is not bare should cover her upper body as well.

Do you want proof of the "authority" that age carries? If so, bring before yourself two females: [a young girl and a woman advanced in age]. Dress the young girl in the clothing of a mature woman. And dress the woman of advanced age in the clothing of a maiden. You will find that you can convince no one that the girl is in fact a woman or that the mature woman is a young virgin. That then is the honesty of *age*. You cannot overcome it even with clothing.

Coming Of Age: A.D. 200

Take note of the fact that these girls of ours testify to their change of age even by their clothing. As soon as they have understood themselves to be women, they withdraw themselves from other girls. They lay aside their former selves, beginning with the head itself. They change the style of their hair and fasten it with more extravagant pins. They profess their obvious womanhood by parting their hair from the front.

Next, they peer into the mirror to enhance their beauty, and they make their overly-detailed faces more slender with washing. Or perhaps they make it beguiling with cosmetics. They toss their hair about them with an air and squeeze their feet into shoes of various shapes. And they carry more paraphernalia to the baths. Why should I go into more detail? They plainly demonstrate their complete womanhood by all of these things. However, they wish to still play the young maiden by the sole fact of leaving their heads bare. They think they can deny by one single matter what they are professing by their entire demeanor.

Wearing The Veil Outdoors

13. If they adopt a false garb on account of men, let them fully carry out that garb even for that purpose. Since they veil their heads in the presence of pagans, let them likewise conceal their virginity in the church. For they do, in fact, veil themselves *outside* the church. Since they fear strangers, let them stand in awe of their brothers too. Or let them be brave enough to appear as virgins in the streets, since they have the boldness to do so in the churches.[t] Identical liberty means there should be the same practice outdoors as there is at home. There should be the same custom in the presence of men as there is in the presence of the Lord.

So what is the purpose of covering their glory when outdoors, but exposing it in the church? I demand a reason! Is it to please the brothers, or to please God himself? If it is to please God, he is capable of seeing whatever is done in secret.

For he is a just God and will repay what is done solely for his honor. In fact, he commands us not to call attention to any of the things we do that would merit reward in his eyes. Nor are we to receive compensation for them from men. We are prohibited from letting our left hand know when we give a single small coin—or any charitable gift whatsoever. (Matt. 6:2,3) Since this is the case, we should enshroud ourselves with the deepest darkness when we offer to God the gift of our very bodies and spirits. That is, when we dedicate our very nature to him.

If we do something contrary to God's way, we are not doing it for *his* sake. And if we do not do something for God's sake, we do it for the sake of men. And something done for the sake of men is wrong, for it betrays a lust for glory. For glory is a thing wrongful to those whose testing consists of humility in every area. And if the virtue of sexual abstinence is conferred by God, then "what do you have that you have not received?" (1 Cor. 4:7) Yet, the fact you do not offer it to God alone shows that it has not been given you *by God*. We shall see, then, whether or not that which is [merely] *human* will prove to be firm and true.

5

Veiling For God's Glory

14. It is reported that when this issue was first debated, someone asked, "How will we be able to persuade the other virgins to follow this same course?" As if it were sheer *numbers* that would bring us joy! Rather, isn't it the grace of God and the merits of each *individual*? Is it the presence of virgins that adorns and commends the Church in the sight of God? Or is it the Church that adorns and commends virgins?

The person who asked this question revealed that the real root of this issue is *glory*. And where there is glory, there is enticement. Where there is enticement, there are physical compulsions. Where there are compulsions, certain actions inevitably follow. And where there are such inevitable actions, there is moral weakness. Ironically, for the sake of "glory," they do not cover their *heads*, but they are later forced to cover their *bellies* in shame because of the ruin [i.e. unwanted pregnancy] resulting from their moral weakness. For what motivates them is not religion, but emulation [of the world].

Virgin Sisterhoods

Or sometimes they are motivated by that god—their stomachs. For the brotherhood readily supplies the needs of virgins.[1] The sad part is that such fallen virgins are not merely

[1]The virgins in a congregation were often supported by the brethren.

personally ruined, but they carry with them "a long rope of sins." (Isa. 5:18) For [when first joining the order of virgins], they are brought forth into the middle of the church. They are elated by the church's approval of their decision [to remain virgin]. And the brethren shower them with all sorts of honors and charitable gifts. However, a virgin receives all of these things only so long as she does not fall [from her virginity].

For that reason, when these virgins do commit immoral sins, they begin to contemplate a deed that is as low as their honors had been high. This deed is as follows: Since an *uncovered* head is a recognized mark of virginity [in some churches], such a fallen virgin permanently goes about with her head uncovered to avoid being discovered. So she walks about in clothing that is designated for another [i.e. a true virgin]. Even though she is surely conscious now of being a *woman*, she has the audacity to approach God with a bare head.

However, the jealous God and Lord will bring such things into public view. For "there is nothing hidden that will not be revealed." (Matt. 10:26) But such women will never confess their sins, unless they are eventually betrayed by an infant's cries.[u] What audacities will such a person do to her womb, for fear of being detected to be [not only a *woman* but] a *mother* as well. God only knows how many infants have been long fought against by their mothers. Yet, he has helped such infants through gestation and development up until they were born sound and whole. Such "virgins" seem to conceive quite readily, have the happiest deliveries, and bear children who are indeed most like their fathers.[v]

Tertullian's Counsel To Virgins

16. In conclusion, I have set forth in this tract the defense of my position. I have demonstrated that my position is in harmony with Scripture, Nature, and Discipline. Scripture establishes the rule. Then Nature attests to the rule. Finally, Discipline requires it. However, which of these three things will support a custom [i.e. not veiling virgins] that is founded

merely on human opinion? What validates their view? For God's rule is validated by Scripture, Nature, and Discipline. Whatever contradicts these three is not from God.

If Scripture is unclear, then Nature is clear. And Scripture is certain about Nature's testimony. (1 Cor. 11:14) If there is doubt about Nature, then Discipline points out what is more approved by God. For nothing is more dear to him than humility. Nothing is more acceptable to him than modesty. Nothing is more offensive to him than self-glory and learning how to please men. Let Scripture, Nature, and Discipline be the basis of your practice, for you will find such to be approved by God. Just as you are invited to "examine all things, and diligently follow whatever is better." (1 Thess. 5:21)

Let me now speak directly to the virgins themselves to persuade them to more willingly accept these suggestions. Permit me to address you according to the terms appropriate for your age—whether it be "mother," "sister," or "virgin daughter." I plead with you to veil your head. If you're a mother, for your sons' sakes. If you're a sister, for your brothers' sakes. If a daughter, for your fathers' sakes.[2] All ages are at risk in your presence. Put on the armor of modesty. Surround yourself with the stockade of quietness. Build a rampart for your femininity that will not allow your eyes access to other people's, or their's to yours.

Wear the full garb of *woman* to preserve your standing as a *virgin*. Disguise somewhat your inward consciousness, in order to exhibit the truth to God alone. Yet, do not deceive yourself in appearing as a bride. For you *are* married—to Christ. To him you have surrendered your flesh. You have given your adulthood in marriage to him. Walk in accordance with the will of your Groom. For Christ is he who commands the wives and engaged virgins *of humans* to veil themselves. And so much more, of course, does he command his own.

---

[2]Tertullian is using the terms, "mother," "sister," "daughter," "sons," "brothers," and "fathers" in a spiritual sense. (1Tim. 5:1,2; Matt. 12:48,49)

Inappropriate Styles Of Head Coverings

17. I also admonish you second group of women, who have fallen into wedlock, not to outgrow the discipline of the veil. Not even for a moment of an hour. Because you can't avoid wearing a veil, you should not find some other way to nullify it. That is, by going about neither covered nor bare. For some women do not *veil* their heads, but rather bind them up with turbans and woollen bands. It's true that they are protected in front. But where the head properly lies, they are bare.

Others cover only the area of the brain with small linen coifs that do not even quite reach the ears. I suppose they adopt this for fear of pressing the head. I feel sorry for them if their hearing is so weak that they can't hear through a covering. They should know that the entire head constitutes the woman. Its limits and boundaries reach as far as the place where the robe begins. The region of the veil is co-extensive with the space covered by the hair when it is unbound. In this way, the neck too is encircled.[w]

The pagan women of Arabia will be your judges. For they cover not only the head, but the face also. They cover it so entirely they have only one eye free. They are content to enjoy only half of the light rather than to prostitute the entire face. Their females would rather see than to be seen. For this reason, a certain Roman queen said that they were most unhappy—in that they could more easily fall in love than be fallen in love with. In truth, they are actually joyful in being immune from the opposite—and indeed more frequent—unhappy situation. For females are more apt to be fallen in love with than to fall in love. And the modesty of pagan discipline is indeed more simple and somewhat more barbaric.

To *us*, through revelations, the Lord has measured the space for the veil to cover. For a certain sister of ours was thus addressed by an angel, clapping her neck, as if in applause. He said to her [in chastisement], "What an elegant neck! And deservedly it is bare. You might as well unveil yourself from the head right down to the loins, otherwise this freedom of the neck doesn't profit you at all." And, of course, what you have said to one, you have said to all.

But how severe a chastisement will *they* likewise deserve, who remain uncovered even during the recital of the Psalms and at any mention of the name of God? For even when they are about to spend time in prayer itself, they only place a fringe, tuft [of cloth], or any thread whatever on the crown of their heads. And they think that they are covered! They falsely imagine their heads to include such a small area.

Others think the palm of their hand is obviously larger than any fringe or thread. Yet, they thereby misuse their head no less.[3] They make me think of a certain winged creature that is more beast than bird. It has a small head and long legs, and it holds itself erect.[4] They say that when this bird needs to hide, it thrusts its entire head—but only its head—in a thicket, leaving the rest of itself exposed. Although it is safe as to its head, it is bare as to the rest of its body. And [the predator] takes all of it, head and body. Thus will be the plight of such women as well, for they cover less than what is prudent.

So at all times, and in every place, we should walk with [God's] law in mind. Thereby, we are prepared and equipped to meet every mention of God. For if he is in the heart of a female, he will be in her head as well.

May peace and grace from our Lord Jesus Christ be with those who read these exhortations with good will and who prefer Truth to Custom. May his peace and grace also be with Septimius Tertullianus, who wrote this tract.

---

[3]These women were apparently simply placing the palms of their hands on their heads as a covering during prayer.

[4]i.e., an ostrich.

Appendix

Passages Omitted From *The Shows*

a. Though if it were, even Christian obstinacy might well give all submission to a plan so suitable, to a rule so excellent.

b. Even though these same works may be carried on by things of His making. For, in fact, it is the one ground of condemnation, that the creature misuses the creation.

c. Who, in our discovery of the Creator, have at the same time laid hands upon the great corrupter.

d. ...in the very thing whose gift to man, but not to him, had grieved him... .

e. In the matter of their origins, as these are somewhat obscure and but little known to many among us, our investigations must go back to a remote antiquity, and our authorities be none other than books of heathen literature. Various authors are extant who have published works on the subject. The origin of the games as given by them is this. Timaeus tells us that immigrants from Asia, under the leadership of Tyrrhenus, who, in a contest about his native kingdom, had succumbed to his brother, settled down in Etruria. Well, among other superstitious observances under the name of religion, they set up in their new home public shows. The Romans, at their own request, obtain from them skilled performers—the proper seasons—the name too, for it is said they are called *Ludi, from Lydi*. And though Varro derives the name of *Ludi* from *Ludus,* that is, from play, as they called the Luperci also *Ludii,* because they ran about making sport; still that sporting of young men belongs, in his view, to festal days and temples, and objects of religious veneration. However, it is of little consequence the origin of the name, when it is certain that the thing springs from idolatry. The Liberalia, under the general designation of Ludi, clearly declared the glory of Father Bacchus; for to Bacchus these festivities were first consecrated by grateful peasants, in return for the boon he conferred on them, as they say, making known the pleasures of wine. Then the Consualia were called *Ludi,* and at first were in honor of Neptune, for Neptune has the name of Consus also. Thereafter Romulus dedicated the Equiria to Mars, though they claim the Consualia too for Romulus, on the ground that he consecrated them to Consus, the god, as they will have it, of counsel; of the counsel, forsooth, in which he planned the rape of the Sabine virgins for wives to his soldiers. An excellent counsel truly; and still I suppose reckoned just and righteous by the Romans themselves, I may not say by God. This goes also to taint the origin: you cannot surely hold that to be good which has sprung from sin, from shamelessness, from violence, from hatred, from a fratricidal founder, from a son of Mars. Even now, at the first turning-post in the circus, there is a subterranean altar to this same Consus, with an inscription to this effect: "Consus, great in counsel, Mars, in battle, mighty tutelar deities." The priests of the state sacrifice at it on the nones of July; the priest of Romulus and the Vestals on the twelfth before the Kalends of September. In addition to this, Romulus instituted games in honor of Jupiter Feretrius on the Tarpeian Hill, according to the statement Piso has handed down to us, called both Tarpeian and Capitoline. After him Numa Pompilius instituted games to Mars and Robigo (for they have also invented a goddess of rust); then Tullus Hostilius; then Ancus Martius; and various others in succession did the like. As to the idols in whose honour these games were established, ample information is to be found in the pages of Suetonius Tranquillus. But we need say no more to prove the accusation of idolatrous origin.

6. To the testimony of antiquity is added that of later games instituted in their turn, and betraying their origin from the titles which they bear even at the present day, in which it is imprinted as on their very face, for what idol and for what religious object games, whether of the one kind or the other, were designed. You have festivals bearing the name of the great Mother and Apollo of Ceres too, and Neptune, and Jupiter Latiaris, and Flora, all celebrated for a common end; the others have their religious origin in the birthdays and solemnities of kings, in public successes in municipal holidays. There are also testamentary exhibitions, in which funeral honors are rendered to the memories of private persons; and this according to an institution of ancient times. For from the first the "Ludi" were regarded as of two sorts, sacred and funereal, that is in honor of the heathen deities and of the dead. But in the matter of idolatry, it makes no difference with us under what name or title it is practised, while it has to do with the wicked spirits whom we abjure. If it is lawful to offer homage to the dead, it will be just as lawful to offer it to their gods: you have the same origin in both cases; there is the same idolatry; there is on our part the same solemn renunciation of all idolatry.

7. The two kinds of public games, then, have one origin; and they have common names, as owning the same parentage. So, too, as they are equally tainted with the sin of idolatry, their foundress, they must needs be like each other in their pomp. But the more ambitious preliminary display of the circus games to which the name procession specially belongs, is in itself the proof to whom the whole thing appertains, in the many images the long line of statues, the chariots of all sorts, the thrones, the crowns, the dresses. What high religious rites besides, what sacrifices precede, come between, and follow. How many guilds, how many priesthoods, how many offices are set astir, is known to the inhabitants of the great city in which the demon convention has its headquarters. If these things are done in humbler style in the provinces, in accordance with their inferior means, still all circus games must be counted as belonging to that from which they are derived; the fountain from which they spring defiles them. The tiny streamlet from its very spring-head, the little twig from its very budding, contains in it the essential nature of its origin. It may be grand or mean, no matter, any circus procession whatever is offensive to God. Though there be few images to grace it, there is idolatry in one; though there be no more than a single sacred car, it is a chariot of Jupiter: anything of idolatry whatever, whether meanly arrayed or modestly rich and gorgeous, taints it in its origin.

8. To follow out my plan in regard to places: the circus is chiefly consecrated to the Sun, whose temple stands in the middle of it, and whose image shines forth from its temple summit; for they have not thought it proper to pay sacred honors underneath a roof to an object they have itself in open space. Those who assert that the first spectacle was exhibited by Circe, and in honor of the Sun her father, as they will have it, maintain also the name of circus was derived from her. Plainly, then, the enchantress did this in the name of the parties whose priestess she was—I mean the demons and spirits of evil. What an aggregation of idolatries you see, accordingly, in the decoration of the place! Every ornament of the circus is a temple by itself. The eggs are regarded as sacred to the Castors, by men who are not ashamed to profess faith in their production from the egg of a swan, which was no other than Jupiter himself. The Dolphins vomit forth in honor of Neptune. Images of Sessia, so called as the goddess of sowing; of Messia, so called as the goddess of reaping; of Tutulina, so called as the fruit-protecting deity—load the pillars. In front of these

you have three altars to these three gods—Great, Mighty, Victorious. They reckon these of Samo-Thrace. The huge Obelisk, as Hermeteles affirms, is set up in public to the Sun; its inscription, like its origin, belongs to Egyptian superstition. Cheerless were the demon-gathering without their Great Mother; and so she presides there over the Euripus. Consus, as we have mentioned, lies hidden under ground at the Murcian Goals. These two sprang from an idol. For they will have it that Murcia is the goddess of love; and to her, at that spot, they have consecrated a temple. See, Christian, how many impure names have taken possession of the circus! You have nothing to do with a sacred place which is tenanted by such multitudes of diabolic spirits. And speaking of places, this is the suitable occasion for some remarks in anticipation of a point that some will raise. What, then, you say; shall I be in danger of pollution if I go to the circus when the games are not being celebrated? There is no law forbidding the mere places to us. For not only the places for show-gatherings, but even the temples, may be entered without any peril of his religion by the servant of God, if he has only some honest reason for it, unconnected with their proper business and official duties. Why, even the streets, and the market-place, and the baths, and the taverns, and our very dwelling-places, are not altogether free from idols. Satan and his angels have filled the whole world. It is not by merely being in the world, however, that we lapse from God, but by touching and tainting ourselves with the world's sins. I shall break with my Maker, that is, by going to the Capitol or the temple of Serapis to sacrifice or adore, as I shall also do by going as a spectator to the circus and the theater. The places in themselves do not contaminate, but what is done in them; from this even the places themselves, we maintain, become defiled. The polluted things pollute us. It is on this account that we set before you to whom places of the kind are dedicated, that we may prove the things which are done in them to belong to the idol-patrons to whom the very places are sacred.

9. Now as to the kind of performances peculiar to the circus exhibitions. In former days equestrianism was practised in a simple way on horseback, and certainly its ordinary use had nothing sinful in it; but when it was dragged into the games, it passed from the service of God into the employment of demons. Accordingly this kind of circus performances is regarded as sacred to Castor and Pollux, to whom, Stesichorus tells us, horses were given by Mercury. And Neptune, too, is an equestrian deity, by the Greeks called Hippius. In regard to the team, they have consecrated the chariot and four to the sun; the chariot and pair to the moon. But, as the poet has it, "Erichthonius first dared to yoke four horses to the chariot, and to ride upon its wheels with victorious swiftness." Erichthonius, the son of Vulcan and Minerva, fruit of unworthy passion upon earth, is a demon-monster, nay, the devil himself, and no mere snake. But if Trochilus the Argive is maker of the first chariot, he dedicated that work of his to Juno. If Romulus first exhibited the four-horse chariot at Rome, he too, I think, has a place given him among idols, at least if he and Quirinus are the same. But as chariots had such inventors, the charioteers were naturally dressed, too, in the colors of idolatry; for at first these were only two, namely white and red,—the former sacred to the winter with its glistening snows, the latter sacred to the summer with its ruddy sun: but afterwards, in the progress of luxury as well as of superstition, red was dedicated by some to Mars, and white by others to the Zephyrs, while green was given to Mother Earth, or spring, and azure to the sky and sea, or autumn. But as idolatry of every kind is condemned by God, that form of it surely shares the condemnation which is offered to the elements of nature.

10. Let us pass on now to theatrical exhibitions, which we have already shown have a common origin with the circus, and bear like idolatrous designations—even as from the first they have borne the name of "Ludi," and equally minister to idols.

They resemble each other also in their pomp, having the same procession to the scene of their display from temples and altars, and that mournful profusion of incense and blood, with music of pipes and trumpets, all under the direction of the soothsayer and the undertaker, those two foul masters of funeral rites and sacrifices. So as we went on from the origin of the "Ludi" to the circus games, we shall now direct our course thence to those of the theater, beginning with the place of exhibition. At first the theater was properly a temple of Venus; and, to speak briefly, it was owing to this that stage performances were allowed to escape censure, and got a footing in the world. For ofttimes the censors, in the interests of morality, put down above all the rising theaters, foreseeing, as they did, that there was great danger of their leading to a general profligacy; so that already, from this accordance of their own people with us, there is a witness to the heathen, and in the anticipatory judgment of human knowledge even a confirmation of our views. Accordingly Pompey the Great, less only than his theater, when he had erected that citadel of all impurities, fearing some time or other censorian condemnation of his memory, superposed on it a temple of Venus; and summoning by public proclamation the people to its consecration, he called it not a theater, but a temple, "under which," said he, "we have placed tiers of seats for viewing the shows." So he threw a veil over a structure on which condemnation had been often passed, and which is ever to be held in reprobation, by pretending that it was a sacred place; and by means of superstition he blinded the eyes of a virtuous discipline. But Venus and Bacchus are close allies. These two evil spirits are in sworn confederacy with each other, as the patrons of drunkenness and lust. So the theater of Venus is as well the house of Bacchus: for they properly gave the name of Liberalia also to other theatrical amusements—which besides being consecrated to Bacchus (as were the Dionysia of the Greeks), were instituted by him; and, without doubt, the performances of the theater have the common patronage of these two deities. That immodesty of gesture and attire which so specially and peculiarly characterizes the stage are consecrated to them—the one deity wanton by her sex, the other by his drapery; while its services of voice, and song, and lute, and pipe, belong to Apollos, and Muses, and Minervas, and Mercuries. You will hate, O Christian, the things whose authors must be the objects of your utter detestation. So we would now make a remark about the arts of the theater, about the things also whose authors in the names we execrate. We know that the names of the dead are nothing, as are their images; but we know well enough, too, who, when images are set up, under these names carry on their wicked work, and exult in the homage rendered to them, and pretend to be divine—none other than spirits accursed, than devils. We see, therefore, that the arts also are consecrated to the service of the beings who dwell in the names of their founders; and that things cannot be held free from the taint of idolatry whose inventors have got a place among the gods for their discoveries. Nay, as regards the arts, we ought to have gone further back, and barred all further argument by the position that the demons, predetermining in their own interests from the first, among other evils of idolatry, the pollutions of the public shows, with the object of drawing man away from his Lord and binding him to their own service, carried out their purpose by bestowing on him the artistic gifts which the shows require. For none but themselves would have made provision and preparation for the objects they had in view; nor would they have given the arts to the world by any but those in whose names, and images, and histories they set up for their own ends the artifice of consecration.

11. In fulfillment of our plan, let us now go on to consider the combats. Their origin is akin to that of the games (*ludi*). Hence they are kept as either sacred or funereal, as they have been instituted in honor of the idol-gods of the nations or of the dead. Thus, too, they are called Olympian in honor of Jupiter, known at Rome as the Capitoline; Nemean, in honor of Hercules; Isthmian, in honor of Neptune; the

rest *mortuarii*, as belonging to the dead. What wonder, then, if idolatry pollutes the combat-parade with profane crowns, with sacerdotal chiefs, with attendants belonging to the various colleges, last of all with the blood of its sacrifices? To add a completing word about the "place"—in the common place for the college of the arts sacred to the Muses, and Apollo, and Minerva, and also for that of the arts dedicated to Mars, they with contest and sound of trumpet emulate the circus in the arena, which is a real temple—I mean of the god whose festivals it celebrates. The gymnastic arts also originated with their Castors, and Herculeses, and Mercuries.

f. To refer also to the matter of names, though this sort of exhibition has passed from honors of the dead to honors of the living, I mean, to quaestorships and magistracies—to priestly offices of different kinds; yet, since idolatry still cleaves to the dignity's name, whatever is done in its name partakes of its impurity. The same remark will apply to the procession of the "Munus," as we look at that in the pomp which is connected with these honors themselves; for the purple robes, the fasces, the fillets, the crowns, the proclamations too, and edicts, the sacred feasts of the day before, are not without the pomp of the devil, without invitation of demons.

g. nay, we do not partake of what is offered either in the one case or the other.

h. In like manner, under the general idea of pleasures, you have as a specific class the "shows." But we have spoken already of how it is with the places of exhibition, that they are not polluting in themselves, but owing to the things that are done in them from which they imbibe impurity, and then spirt it again on others. (15.) Having done enough, then, as we have said, in regard to that principal argument, that there is in them all the taint of idolatry—having sufficiently dealt with that...

i. What are the partakers in all this—not their own masters— to obtain of it for themselves? Unless, it may be, that which makes them not their own: they are saddened by another's sorrow, they are gladdened by another's joy. Whatever they desire on the one hand, or detest on the other, is entirely foreign to themselves. So love with them is a useless thing, and hatred is unjust.

j. Which finally is done from his childhood on the person of the pantomime, that he may become an actor.

k. And you will have the very opposite of complacency in the athletes Greece, in the inactivity of peace, feeds up.

l. So much the more cruel he if that was not his wish.

m. ...and have been got up entirely with the devil's things (for all that is not God's, or is not pleasing in His eyes, belongs to His wicked rival)...

n. Nay, in the whole thing he will meet with no greater temptation than that gay attiring of the men and women. [apparently spoken rhetorically]

o. And there are even more sights. There is the last day of judgment, with its everlasting judgments. Think also of that day not looked for by the nations—the day that is the theme of their derision. I speak of the day when the world and its elements—hoary with age—will be consumed in one great flame. (2 Pet. 3:10) How vast a spectacle will then burst upon the eye! What there excites my admiration? What incites my derision? What sight gives me joy? What rouses me to exultation?

The famous kings of this earth have already been publicly announced to have been received in the heavens. Yet, on that day I will see these kings groaning in the lowest darkness with the great Jupiter himself. They will be there along with those who bore witness of their rise to heaven.

With them also will be those provincial governors who persecuted the name "Christian." They will be there in fires more fierce than those they raged against the followers of Christ in the days of their pride. There too will be the wise men of the world and the philosophers themselves. For they taught their followers that God had no interest in earthly things. They told them that either humans have no souls, or else that our souls will never return to the bodies we leave behind at death. On that day, there they will sit in abashment, along with their poor deluded students, as the same fire consumes them all.

The poets will be there too. But they won't be trembling before the judgment seat of Rhadamanthys or Minos. No, they will tremble before the seat of Christ, whom they did not expect. On that day, I will have opportunity enough to hear the tragic actors, who will be even louder voiced in their calamity. Then, will I be able to see the stage actors, who will be more dissolute in the dissolving flame. At that time I will behold the charioteer, all glowing in his chariot of fire. I will see the wrestlers, not in the gymnasium, but tossing in the billowing flames.

Yet, probably even then, I will have little interest in watching *those* servants of sin. Instead, I will no doubt be eager to intently gaze on those who vented their fury on the Lord. "This," I shall say, "this is that 'carpenter's son!' That 'hireling's son!' That 'Sabbath breaker!' That 'Samaritan' and 'demon-possessed man!' This is he whom you purchased from Judas! This is he whom you struck with reed and fist. This is he whom you contemptuously spat upon! This is he whom you gave gall and vinegar to drink! This is he whom 'his disciples secretly stole away, so it could be said that he had risen. Or, the gardener abstracted, that his lettuces might come to no harm from the crowds of visitants!"

Passages Omitted From *On Prayer*

a. Further, since wisdom succeeded in the following precept, let it in like manner appertain unto faith.

b. Because it is equally due to the sentence of judgment, and is exacted by it.

c. That they may themselves participate in our observance, and thereby be mollified for transacting with their brother touching their own peace.

d. …men of no consideration whatever….

e. (22.) They who make this concession ought to reflect on the nature of the word itself—what is the meaning of 'woman' from the very first records of the sacred writings. Here they find it to be the name of the sex, not a class of the sex: if, that is, God gave to Eve, when she had not yet known a man, the surname "woman" and "female"—("female," whereby the sex generally; "woman," whereby a class of the sex, is marked). So, since at that time the as yet unwedded Eve was called by the word "woman," that word has been made common even to a virgin. Nor is it wonderful that the apostle—guided, of course, by the same Spirit by whom, as all the divine Scripture, so that book Genesis, was drawn up—has used the selfsame word in writing "women," which, by the example of Eve unwedded, is applicable too to a "virgin." In fact, all the other passages are in consonance herewith. For even by this very fact, that he has not named "virgins" (as he does in another place where he is teaching touching marrying), he sufficiently predicates that his remark is made touching every woman, and touching the whole sex; and that there is no distinction made between a "virgin" and any other, while he does not name her at all. For he who elsewhere—namely, where the difference requires—remembers to make the distinction, (moreover, he makes it by designating each species by their appropriate names,) wishes, where he makes no distinction (while he does not name each), no difference to be understood. What of the fact that in the Greek speech, in which the apostle wrote his letters, it is usual to say, "women" rather than "females;" that is, *gynaikas* rather than *theleias*? Therefore if that word, which by interpretation represents what "female" (*femina*) represents, is frequently used instead of the name of the sex, he has named the sex in saying *gynaikas*; but in the sex even the virgin is embraced. But, withal, the declaration is plain: "Every woman," saith he, "praying and prophesying with head uncovered, dishonoureth her own head." What is "every woman," but woman of every age, of every rank, of every condition? By saying "every" he excepts nought of womanhood, just as he excepts nought of manhood either from not being covered; for just so he says, "every man." As, then, in the masculine sex, under the name of "man" even the "youth" is forbidden to be veiled; so, too, in the feminine, under the name of "woman," even the "virgin" is bidden to be veiled. Equally in each sex let the younger age follow the discipline of the elder; or else let the male "virgins," too, be veiled, if the female virgins withal are not veiled, because they are not mentioned by name. Let "man" and "youth" be different, if "woman" and "virgin" are different. For indeed it is "on account of the angels" that he saith women must be veiled, because on account of "the daughters of men" angels revolted from God. Who, then, would contend that "women" alone—that is, such as were already wedded and had lost their virginity—were the objects of angelic concupiscence, unless "virgins" are incapable of excelling in beauty and finding lovers? Nay, let us see whether it were not virgins alone whom they lusted after; since Scriptures saith "the daughters of men;" inasmuch as it might have named "wives of men," or "females," indifferently. Likewise, in that it saith, "And they took them to themselves for wives," it does so on this ground, that, of course, such are "received for wives" as are devoid of that title. But it would have expressed itself differently concerning such as were not thus devoid. And so (they who are named) are devoid as much of widowhood as of virginity. So completely has Paul by naming the sex generally, mingled "daughters" and species together in the genus. Again, while he says that "nature herself," which has assigned hair as a tegument and ornament to woman, "teaches that veiling is the duty of females," has not the same tegument and the same honor of the head been assigned also to virgins? If "it is shameful" for a woman to be shorn it is similarly so to a virgin too. From them, then, to whom is assigned one and the same law of the head, one and the same discipline of the head is exacted,— (which extends) even unto those virgins whom their childhood defends, for from the first a virgin was named "female." This custom, in short, even Israel observes; but if Israel did not observe it, our Law, amplified and supplemented, would vindicate the addition for itself; let it be excused for imposing the veil on virgins also. Under our dispensation, let that age which is ignorant of its sex retain the privilege of simplicity. For both Eve and Adam, when it befell them to be "wise," forthwith veiled what they had learned to know. At all events, with regard to those in whom girlhood has changed (into maturity), their age ought to remember its duties as to nature, so also, to discipline; for they are being transferred to the rank of "women" both in their persons and in their functions. No one is a "virgin" from the time when she is capable of marriage; seeing that, in her, age has by that time been wedded to its own husband, that is, to time. "But some particular virgin has devoted herself to God. From that very moment she both changes the fashion of her hair, and converts all her garb into that of a 'woman.'" Let her, then, maintain the character wholly, and perform the whole function of a "virgin:" what she conceals for the sake of God, let her cover quite over. It is our business to entrust to the knowledge of God alone that which the grace of God effects in us, lest we receive from man the reward we hope for from God. Why do you denude before God what you cover before men? Will you be more modest in public than in the church? If your self-devotion is a grace of God, and you have received it, "why do you boast," saith he, "as if you have not received it?" Why, by your ostentation of yourself, do you judge others? Is it that, by your boasting, you invite others unto good? Nay, but even you yourself run the risk of losing, if you boast; and you drive others unto the same perils? What is assumed from love of boasting is easily destroyed. Be veiled, virgin, if virgin you are; for you ought to blush. If you are a virgin, shrink from (the gaze of) many eyes. Let no one wonder at your face; let no one perceive your falsehood. You do well in falsely assuming the married character, if you veil your head; nay, you do not seem to assume it falsely, for you are wedded to Christ: to Him you have surrendered your body; act as becomes your Husband's discipline. If He bids the brides of others to be veiled, His own, of course, much more. "But each individual man is not to think that the institution of his predecessor is to be overturned." Many yield up their own judgment, and its consistency, to the custom of others. Granted that virgins be not compelled to be veiled, at all events such as voluntarily are so should not be prohibited; who, likewise, cannot deny themselves to be virgins, content, in the security of a good conscience before God, to damage their own fame. Touching such, however, as are betrothed, I can with constancy "above my small measure" pronounce and attest that they are to be veiled from that day forth on which they shuddered at the first bodily touch of a man by kiss and hand. For in them everything has been forewedded: their age, through maturity; their flesh, through age; their spirit, through consciousness; their modesty, through the experience of the kiss; their hope, through expectation; their mind, through volition. And Rebecca is example enough for us, who, when her betrothed had been pointed out, veiled herself for marriage merely on recognition of him.

f. Making their breath vibrate after their own manner.

Passages Omitted From *On The Apparel Of Women*

a. ...although it be actively tenacious of itself in the mind up to a certain point....

b. First, because the study of making personal grace (which we know to be naturally the inviter of lust) a mean of pleasing does not spring from a sound conscience.

c. Secondly, because we ought not to open a way to temptations, which, by their instancy, sometimes achieve a wickedness which God expels from them who are His; or, at all events, put the spirit into a thorough tumult by presenting a stumbling-block to it.

d. Which concupiscence, if God, in "amplifying the law," do not dissociate in the way of penalty from the actual commission of fornication.

e. Are women who think that, in furnishing to their neighbor that which is demanded of beauty, they are furnishing it to themselves also, to augment that beauty when naturally given them, and to strive after it when not thus given?

f. To us, in the first place, there is no studious pursuit of "glory," because "glory" is the essence of exaltation. Now exaltation is incongruous for professors of humility according to God's precepts. Secondly, if all "glory" is "vain" and insensate, how much more glory in the flesh, especially to us? For even if "glorying" is allowable, we ought to wish our sphere of pleasing to lie in the graces of the Spirit, not in the flesh; because we are "suitors" of things spiritual. In those things wherein our sphere of labor lies, let your joy lie. From the sources whence we hope for salvation, let us cull our "glory."

g. But, if the self-same angels who disclosed both the material substances of this kind and their charms—of gold, I mean, and lustrous stones—and taught men how to work them, and by and by instructed them...

Passages Omitted From *On Baptism*

a. I am a deceiver if, on the contrary, it is not from their circumstance, and preparation, and expense, that [pagan] idols' solemnities or mysteries get their credit and authority built up.

b. But it is the more to be believed if the wonderfulness be the reason why it is *not* believed.

c. God is wise and powerful: even those who pass him by do not deny that. So it is with good reason that he lays the foundations of his own operation in what is contrary to wisdom and power (that is, in foolishness and impossibility). Every virtue receives its cause from those things which called it forth.

d. Which (earth) "the waters," separated the fourth day before into their own place, temper with their remaining moisture to a clay-like consistency. If, from that time onward, I [could] continue in recounting universally, or at more length, ...

e. This was even then fore-noted by the very attitude assumed for a type of baptism.

f. For it is necessary that in every case an underlying material substance should catch the quality of that which overhangs it, most of all a corporeal of a spiritual, adapted (as the spiritual is) through the subtlety of its substance, both for penetrating and insinuating.

g. But this, like the former, is derived from the old sacred ceremony in which Jacob blessed his grandsons, born of Joseph, Ephraim, and Manasseh. With his hands laid on them and interchanged, and indeed so transversely slanted one over the other, that, by delineating Christ, they even portended the future benediction into Christ.

h. Especially then, if there were any one to whom they clung, the Lord had exalted John above him by the testimony saying, "Among those who are born of women there is none greater than John the Baptist." [Matt 11:11]

i. ...in which case the saying of the Lord concerning the "one bath" does, under the person of Peter, merely apply to *us* [not the apostles]...

j. The comparison with this law of that definition.

k. Nor is that capable of being counted which is not had. So they cannot receive it either, because they do not have it.

l. For then the steadfast courage of the one who succors, when the situation of the endangered one is urgent, is exceptionally admissible.

m. ...as if he were augmenting Paul's fame from his own storehouse,...

n. Every "petition" may both deceive and be deceived.

o. For no less cause must the unwedded also be deferred—in whom the ground of temptation is prepared, alike in such as never were wedded by means of their maturity, and in the widowed by means of their freedom—until they either marry, or else be fully strengthened for continence.

Passages Omitted From *On The Veiling Of Virgins*

a. ...from some ignorance or simplicity.

b. On the other hand, if any is ignorant of anything, the ignorance proceeds from his own defect. Moreover, whatever is matter of ignorance ought to have been as carefully inquired into as whatever is matter of acknowledgment received.

c. But above, withal, He made a declaration concerning this his work.

d. And antecedently, I think, to certain founders, who shall be nameless.

e. Because the front of sin is more hard, learning shamelessness from and in the sin itself.

f. ...so that the licence granted to either fashion was becoming the mean whereby the indication of the better part emerged...

g. And the semblance of virgins is exhibited by women who have the power of asking somewhat from husbands, not to say such a request as that forsooth their rivals—all the more "free" in that they are the "handmaids" of Christ alone—may be surrendered to them.

h. Naturally, a compendious style of speech is both pleasing and necessary; inasmuch as diffuse speech is both tiresome and vain. So, too, we are content with general words, which comprehend in themselves the understanding of the specialties.

i. Because the general is prior; and the succedent to the antecedent, and the partial to the universal. Each is implied in the word itself to which it is subject; and is signified in it because is contained in it.

j. But what kind of hypothesis is it that one who, with an eye to the future, was called by a definite name, at the present time should have nothing for a surname?

k. Called as each nature was by that to which from the beginning it showed a propensity.

l. ...just as it has thus educed many other things too which we shall elsewhere be able to show to derive from the Scriptures the origin of their doing and saying...

m. Having therefore settled the name of the newly-made female— which name is woman—and having explained what she formerly was, that is, having sealed the name to her, he immediately turned to the prophetic reason, so as to say.... ."

n. Thus in this case too it is shown, that it was not from a future circumstance that she was at that time named "woman," who was shortly after to receive the name which would be proper to her future condition.

o. For elsewhere, we grant, we must thus hold.

p. As having been called by this name from the beginning: for that must necessarily have a prejudicating force from which the normal type has descended. Else, as far as relates to the present passage, if Mary is here put on a level with a "betrothed" ...

q. Here, at all events, there can be no semblance of speaking prophetically, as if the apostle should have named a future woman, that is, a bride, in saying that He was "made of a 'woman.'" For he could not be naming a posterior woman, from whom Christ had not to be born—that is, one who had known a man; but she who was then present, who was a virgin, was withal called a woman in consequence of the propriety of this name— vindicated, in accordance with the primordial norm, as belonging to a virgin, and thus to the universal class of women.

r. Therefore, if the fact that it is said "every *man*" makes it plain that the name of man is common even to him who is not yet a man, a stripling male; if, moreover, since the name is common according to nature, the law of not veiling him who among men is a virgin is common too according to discipline: why is it that it is not consequently prejudged that, woman being named, every female virgin is similarly comprised in the fellowship of the name, so to be comprised too in the community of the law?

s. [This is] through the common pledge of conscience whereby they mutually plighted their whole confusion. How much more will time veil them? Time—without which they cannot be espoused. And by whose urgency, without espousals, they cease to be virgins.

t. I will praise their vigour, if they succeed in selling aught of virginity among the heathens withal.

u. But, in so far as they are "more numerous," will you not just have them suspected of the more crimes? I will say (albeit I would rather not) it is a difficult thing for one to turn *woman* once for all who fears to do so, and who, when already so turned (in secret) has the power of (still) falsely pretending to be a *virgin* under the eye of God.

v. These crimes does a forced and unwilling virginity incur. The very concupiscence of non-concealment is not modest: it experiences somewhat which is no mark of a virgin,—the study of pleasing, of course, ay, and (of pleasing) men. Let her strive as much as you please with an honest mind; she must necessarily be imperilled by the public exhibition of herself, while she is penetrated by the gaze of untrustworthy and multitudinous eyes, while she is tickled by pointing fingers, while she is too well loved, while she feels a warmth creep over her amid assiduous embraces and kisses. Thus the forehead hardens; thus the sense of shame wears away; thus it relaxes; thus is learned the desire of pleasing in another way!

(15.) Nay, but true and absolute and pure virginity fears nothing more than itself. Even female eyes it shrinks from encountering. Other eyes itself has. It betakes itself for refuge to the veil of the head as to a helmet, as to a shield, to protect its glory against the blows of temptations, against the darts of scandals, against suspicions and whispers and emulation; (against) envy also itself. For there is a something even among the heathens to be apprehended, which they call Fascination, the too unhappy result of excessive praise and glory. This we sometimes interpretatively ascribe to the devil, for of him comes hatred of good; sometimes we attribute it to God, for of Him comes judgment upon haughtiness, exalting, as He does, the humble, and depressing the elated. The more holy virgin, accordingly, will fear, even under the name of fascination, on the one hand the adversary, on the other God,—the envious disposition of the former, the censorial light of the latter; and will joy in being known to herself alone and to God. But even if she has been recognized by any other, she is wise to have blocked up the pathway against temptations. For who will have the audacity to intrude with his eyes upon a shrouded face? A face without feeling? A face, so to say, morose? Any evil cogitation whatsoever will be broken by the very severity. She who conceals her virginity, by that fact denies even her womanhood.

w. For it is they which must be subjected, for the sake of which "power" ought to be "had on the head": the veil is their yoke.

Index